ON A SNOWY DAY

- The 8 Secret Blessings and Inspirations of the Snowy Day

This Book was presented to

_____

on the <u>11th</u> of <u>August 2013</u>

by

<u>RCCG Fountain of Love</u>

ERRATA

The following editorial corrections were late for the printing process, but will Be corrected in the second printing/edition

PAGE	CORRECTION
13	"snowy day" is rendered as "swondy day" in certain references
15	"Geographic" is rendered as "Geographhic"
23	"that are of" is rendered as "that of"
24	"floodgates of heaven" is rendered as "floodgate of snow"
32	"time" is rendered as "tine"
40	"confirmation of God's" is rendered as "confirmation of the God's"
40	"cannot be" is rendered as "cannot be by"
49	"normal again" is rendered as "normal human again"
51	"and" is rendered as "sand"
55	"will" is rendered as "ill"
56	"left" is rendered as "lef"
54	"food" is rendered as "doors"
57	"Church do not" is rendered as "Church I do not"
61	"work out" is rendered as "work with"
65	"parable says" is rendered as "parable man says"
70	"bible says the" is rendered as "bible says that"
71	"It is for" is rendered as "it for"
81	"in" is repeated
88	"from a" is rendered as "from an"
88	"In a short space" is rendered as "in short space"
89	"how did this" is rendered as "how did they"
89	"it was as" is repeated
94	"winter" is rendered as "winters"
99	"that in the united kingdom" is rendered as "that the in"
100	"starts off" is rendered as "starts of"
100	"Nation" is rendered as "Nations"
106	"little" is preferred to "wee" (which is Doric for small or little)
107	"the" is repeated
111	"it" is repeated
117	"by God to" is rendered as "by God and"
119	"for children" is rendered as "from children"
123	"from Moses's experience" is rendered as "from Moses"
124	"Moses offended" is rendered as "Moses offended against"
125	"it is more" is rendered as "it is a more"
130	"that" is repeated
141	"Comfortable at home" is rendered as "comfortable at home and Comfortable"
152	"God" is rendered as "od"

Enter into the amazing blessings awaiting you…

ON A SNOWY DAY

The 8 Secret Blessings and Inspirations of the Snowy Day

"Two Books in One"

Dr Mark Osa Igiehon

School of Wisdom
Aberdeen

SCHOOL OF WISDOM

...

EIGHT SECRET BLESSINGS AND INSPIRATIONS OF THE SNOWY DAY

...

© DR MARK OSAYOMWANBO IGIEHON

...

PUBLISHED IN 2012
BY THE SCHOOL OF WISDOM

...

ISBN: 978-1-908327-03-1

...

...

Cover Design/Typesetting/Printing by
The Vine Media Comm. Ltd
Tel: +44 (0) 7852 216 366

The School of Wisdom will love to hear about your experiences, insights and testimonies.

Please contact us at
School of Wisdom
13 Smithfield Road,
Aberdeen AB24 4NR
email: info@cogcampus.org
Tel: +44.1224.588884,
+44.1224.484.634

CONTENTS

BOOK 1
The Eight Secret Blessings of the Snowy Day

BOOK 2
Benaiah and the Snowy Day Crew and other stories of Snowy Inspiration

BOOK ONE

THE EIGHT SECRET BLESSINGS AND INSPIRATIONS OF THE SNOWY DAY

12

PROLOGUE

*S*ecrets of the Snowy day are for anyone to learn and draw inspiration from,- whether they have seen snow or not. There are secrets and inspirations for victorious living, secrets of change and transformation and secrets beyond the visible, written into the snow and the snowdy day..

The snowy day is an amazing day beyond any imagination. The snowy day is a series of parables and evidence of the divine. For example, if you desire life or situation to be changed instantaneously, in one day, month, or year, consider how God He uses the snow to transform the landscape instantaneously.

What do we do with the snow? What happens on a snowy day?

Enjoy the inspirations, insights, challenges and stories of exploits written into the snowy day.

Now unto him that is able to do exceeding abundantly above all that we ask or think, according to the power that worketh in us, be glory forever. (Eph.3:20).

FIRST SECRET

EARTH IN TROUBLE, HEAVEN OKAY!

*The Snowy Day is parable and physical confirmation of
Heaven's promises always kept!*

*While the earth remaineth, seedtime and harvest,
and cold and heat, and summer and winter,
and day and night shall not cease (Gen. 8:22).*

Rains that are almost biblical,
Heat waves that don't' end,
Tornadoes that strike in savage swarms –
There's been a change in the weather
Lately. What's going on?
Weather gone Wild

That was National Geraphhic describing the new weather patterns across the world. Extreme weather once described as once-in-a-century are becoming common place. Once-in-millennium storms, hurricanes, tsunamis, droughts and other extreme weather occurrences, are now happening with frequency. While extreme and unusual rain storms, tsunamis and the like are happening with regularity in parts of the world, other parts – such as Texas, Australia, Russia and East Africa are suffering severe droughts of biblical dimensions. There is general consensus that the trend of regularly occurring unusual weather is in part, due to *a dangerous, human-made shift in Earth's climate.*

Global warming is real: the earth is getting warmed up. Nothing unusual about that since right from the days of Adam to date, man has always exhibited the tendency to abuse and misuse the earthly resources provided by God. So no surprise about global warming!

Yet while the earth may be in trouble from increasing unusual and extreme weather patterns – tremendous increase in the occurrences of hurricanes, tsunamis, God's promises never fail.

> *While the earth remaineth, seedtime and harvest, and cold and heat, and summer and winter, and day and night shall not cease (Gen. 8:22).*

Global warming or no global warming, wintertime will continue as confirmation of God's word. And that's why you can look at the snow and *know that the word of God will never fail. The word of God says that as long as the earth remains, there would be summer and winter.*

When you see the snow, it gives you that great assurance that the promises of God never change. There may be all kinds of things happening in the world's weather and the finances and resources of Government, but as long as the earth remains, God will not fail you. The Bible says summer and winter will not cease, and He is bringing to pass in your life the promises of more than 6,000 years!

What is that promise that you are expecting from the Lord? Despite the global warming, and what men have said about the ozone depletion, global warming, if God did not fail concerning the consistency of the winter pattern, God will not fail to keep His promise concerning you.

He is an unchanging God. Men, weather and times may change but He never changes. That's why it is so basic common sense to align yourself with the ever faithful and unchanging God.

> *God is our refuge and strength, A very present help in trouble. Therefore will we not fear, though the earth do change, And though the mountains be shaken into the heart of the seas;*

> *Though the waters thereof roar and be troubled, Though the mountains tremble with the swelling thereof. [Selah] There is a river, the streams whereof*

make glad the city of God, The holy place of the tabernacles of the Most High. God is in the midst of her; She shall not be moved: God will help her, and that right early. The nations raged, the kingdoms were moved: He uttered his voice, the earth melted. Jehovah of hosts is with us; The God of Jacob is our refuge. [Selah] Come, behold the works of Jehovah, What desolations he hath made in the earth. He maketh wars to cease unto the end of the earth; He breaketh the bow, and cutteth the spear in sunder; He burneth the chariots in the fire. Be still, and know that I am God: I will be exalted among the nations, I will be exalted in the earth.Jehovah of hosts is with us; The God of Jacob is our refuge. [Selah] (Ps 46 ASV)

The earth may be in trouble but Heaven is always fine. It is always fine with everyone and everything birthed or connected with Heaven. The snowy day is a parable, a physical confirmation of Heaven's promises always kept! Blessed therefore is everyone who has a connection to Heaven. For everything in, with or connected to Heaven will always turn out well. *And we know all things work out together to them who love God, to them who are the called according to His purpose or good for those are called by God according to His purpose. (Ro 8.28)*

And we know that to them that love God all things work together for good, even to them that are called according to his purpose. For whom he foreknew, he also foreordained to be conformed to the image of his

Son, that he might be the firstborn among many brethren: 30 and whom he foreordained, them he also called: and whom he called, them he also justified: and whom he justified, them he also glorified.

What then shall we say to these things? If God is for us, who is against us? He that spared not his own Son, but delivered him up for us all, how shall he not also with him freely give us all things? Who shall lay anything to the charge of God's elect? It is God that justifieth; who is he that condemneth? It is Christ Jesus that died, yea rather, that was raised from the dead, who is at the right hand of God, who also maketh intercession for us. Who shall separate us from the love of Christ? shall tribulation, or anguish, or persecution, or famine, or nakedness, or peril, or sword? Even as it is written, For thy sake we are killed all the day long; We were accounted as sheep for the slaughter.

Nay, in all these things we are more than conquerors through him that loved us. For I am persuaded, that neither death, nor life, nor angels, nor principalities, nor things present, nor things to come, nor powers, nor height, nor depth, nor any other creature, shall be able to separate us from the love of God, which is in Christ Jesus our Lord. (Ro 8 ASV)

SECOND SECRET

MEN AND GOVERNMENTS RUN OUT OF RESOURCES - NATIONS, EMPIRES AND CIVILISATIONS END - BUT HEAVEN'S INEXHAUSTIBLE RESOURCES NEVER RUN OUT

The Snowy Day is parable and physical confirmation of the inexhaustibility of Heaven's resources and storehouses

Hast thou entered into the treasures of the snow? Or hast thou seen the treasure of the hail? (Job 38:22)

Europe has seen a lot of winters and experienced several severe snowfalls since records began. Usually in many parts, snow stays on the ground for four or five days before being washed away. But in the winters of 2009/2010 and 2010/2011, the winter persisted and continuous snowfall was recorded in some places for more than four weeks running. In many parts, Government agencies ran out of resources to keep the roads cleared and under control.

> *Woe to them that go down to Egypt for help; and stay on horses, and trust in chariots, because they are many; and in horsemen, because they are very strong; but they look not unto the Holy One of Israel, neither seek the LORD (Isaiah 31:1)*

If you trust a man for resources, one day, he will run out of it. If you put your trust in governments, some day or another, the government will run out of or withdraw those particular resources or itself will run out of life. Many countries in the West are in the deepest throes of recession – governments across many countries have themselves ran out of financial resources, ethical and moral compasses. For the banks who lend capital, many have gone bankrupt and out of business. Recession is of the epic type described in Scripture as famine. Leadership is failing the populations.

Through all this, I discovered something wonderful in the Scriptures. We see that snow is something God has made for which we should be grateful; and the fact of Europe seeing the coldest winter in 30 years and the most significant overflow of snow in generations, is a blessing and privilege to see. For there is a confirmation of God's remembrance and God's inexhaustible supply of goodness and resources. The snow does not just come from anywhere, it comes from God's storehouse.

> *Hast thou entered into the treasures of the snow? Or*
> *hast thou seen the treasure of the hail? (Job 38:22)*

We therefore understand that there is a special place where snow comes from. Snow comes from the storehouses of heaven! And the storehouses of heaven are inexhaustible, they never run dry like the storehouses of men and government do during recession, and famine.

As Heaven has storehouses and inexhaustible storehouses of snow, so God has other storehouses that of all types of goodness, blessings and resources pertaining to life and godliness. God also has storehouses where weapons for fighting His enemies are kept against the day of battle. That confirms that there is abundance in everything God has. God's resources are never at risk of running flat like those of men, banks and governments are doing. His resources are inexhaustible.

> *For every beast of the forest is mine, and the cattle upon*
> *a thousand hills. I know all the fowls of the mountains:*
> *and the wild beasts of the field are mine. If I were hungry,*
> *I would not tell thee: for the world is mine, and the*
> *fullness thereof. (Ps 50.10-12)*

1. God has great store houses in heaven which comprise of peace – He says He gives you the kind of peace which the world cannot give;

2. Great storehouses of blessings – James 1:17 says every good and perfect gift comes from God.
3. Storehouses of healing, fruitfulness, babies, wealth
4. Heaven's resources can be dispensed in dimensions corresponding to window measures, rain measures and flood measures.
5. Not only does heaven have great storehouse, from time to time, the resources are poured out in tremendous flow and flood akin to the opening of floodgates.
6. When God opens the floodgates of snow, the barren will have children, the spinster will get married, etc. Once a friend asked the Lord in prayers for a husband and bewildering number of suitors came for her hand in marriage – floodgates of suitors. Her challenge became how to make the right choice under God..

When you see the snow, you see the physical demonstration of the abundance of Heaven's resources and supply. And the good news is that Heaven's resources are available to you to access in whatever measures you desire! Small portions? Window-size portions? Overflowing size portions? Floodgate-size portions?

One year, we trusted the Lord as a Church for *Ever-increasing Increase* and we saw increases of incredible proportions. A dear family testified that the career increase they long awaited came in that year - and when it came, they described it as "catapulting promotion". For someone reading this, it is time for you to receive your catapulting increase!

God's power and ability is incredible and terrifying. All that power and ability is available for the good of mankind. The most wise of scientists understand only a small dimension of God's wonderful earth and creation. Science which can be described as man discovering what God has done, cannot yet unravel the fullness of the mystery of God's creation. The great scientist Isaac Newton who discovered the principle of gravity was smart to put the discovery in divine context: *"Gravity explains the motions of the planets, but it cannot explain who set the planets in motion. God governs all things and knows all that is or can be done".*

Some of the mystery of the earth is described in Job thus:

And the Lord made answer to Job out of the storm- wind, and said, Who is this who makes the purpose of God dark by words without knowledge? Get your strength together like a man of war; I will put questions to you, and you will give me the answers.

Where were you when I put the earth on its base? Say, if you have knowledge. By whom were its measures fixed? Say, if you have wisdom; or by whom was the line stretched out over it? On what were its pillars based, or who put down its angle- stone, When the morning stars made songs together, and all the sons of the gods gave cries of joy? Or where were you when the sea came to birth, pushing out from its secret place; When I made the cloud its robe, and put thick clouds as bands round it, Ordering a fixed limit for it, with locks and doors; And said, So far you may come, and no farther; and here the pride of your waves will be stopped?

Have you, from your earliest days, given orders to the morning, or made the dawn conscious of its place; So that it might take a grip of the skirts of the earth, shaking all the evil- doers out of it? It is changed like wet earth under a stamp, and is coloured like a robe; And from the evil- doers their light is kept back, and the arm of pride is broken. 16 Have you come into the springs of the sea, walking in the secret places of the deep?

Have the doors of death been open to you, or have the door- keepers of the dark ever seen you? Have you taken note of the wide limits of the earth? Say, if you have knowledge of it all. Which is the way to the resting- place of the light, and where is the store- house of the dark; So that you might take it to its limit, guiding it to its house? No doubt you have knowledge of it, for then you had come to birth, and the number of your days is great.

Have you come into the secret place of snow, or have you seen the store- houses of the ice- drops, Which I have kept for the time of trouble, for the day of war and fighting? Which is the way to the place where the wind is measured out, and the east wind sent out over the earth? By whom has the way been cut for the flowing of the rain, and the flaming of the thunder; Causing rain to come on a land where no man is living, on the waste land which has no people; To give water to the land where there is waste and destruction, and to make the dry land green with young grass?

Has the rain a father? or who gave birth to the drops of night mist? Out of whose body came the ice? and who gave birth to the cold mist of heaven? The waters are joined together, hard as a stone, and the face of the deep is covered. Are the bands of the Pleiades fixed by you, or are the cords of Orion made loose? Do you make Mazzaroth come out in its right time, or are the Bear and its children guided by you?

Have you knowledge of the laws of the heavens? did you give them rule over the earth? Is your voice sent up to the cloud, so that you may be covered by the weight of waters? Do you send out the thunder- flames, so that they may go, and say to you, Here we are? Who has put wisdom in the high clouds, or given knowledge to the lights of the north? By whose wisdom are the clouds numbered, or the water- skins of the heavens turned to the earth, When the earth becomes hard as metal, and is joined together in masses?

Do you go after food for the she- lion, or get meat so that the young lions may have enough, When they are stretched out in their holes, and are waiting in the brushwood? Who gives in the evening the meat he is searching for, when his young ones are crying to God; when the young lions with loud noise go wandering after their food?

Have you knowledge of the rock- goats? or do you see the roes giving birth to their young? Is the number of their months fixed by you? or is the time when they give birth ordered by you? They are bent down, they give birth to their young, they let loose the fruit of their body. Their young ones are strong, living in the open country; they go out and do not come back again.

Who has let the ass of the fields go free? or made loose the bands of the loud- voiced beast? To whom I have given the waste land for a heritage, and the salt land as a living- place. He makes sport of the noise of the town; the voice of the driver does not come to his ears; He goes looking for his grass- lands in the mountains, searching out every green thing.

Will the ox of the mountains be your servant? or is his night's resting- place by your food- store? Will he be pulling your plough with cords, turning up the valleys after you? Will you put your faith in him, because his strength is great? will you give the fruit of your work into his care? Will you be looking for him to come back, and get in your seed to the crushing- floor?

Is the wing of the ostrich feeble, or is it because she has no feathers, That she puts her eggs on the earth, warming them in the dust, Without a thought that they may be crushed by the foot, and broken by the beasts of the field? She is cruel to her young ones, as if they were not hers; her work is to no purpose; she has no fear. For God has taken wisdom from her mind, and given her no measure of knowledge. When she is shaking her wings on high, she makes sport of the horse and of him who is seated on him.

Do you give strength to the horse? is it by your hand that his neck is clothed with power? Is it through you that he is shaking like a locust, in the pride of his loud-sounding breath? He is stamping with joy in the valley; he makes sport of fear. In his strength he goes out against the arms of war, turning not away from the sword. The bow is sounding against him; he sees the shining point of spear and arrow. Shaking with passion, he is biting the earth; he is not able to keep quiet at the sound of the horn; When it comes to his ears he says, Aha! He is smelling the fight from far off, and hearing the thunder of the captains, and the war- cries.

Is it through your knowledge that the hawk takes his flight, stretching out his wings to the south? Or is it by your orders that the eagle goes up, and makes his resting-place on high? On the rock is his house, and on the mountain- top his strong place. From there he is watching for food; his eye sees it far off. His young have blood for their drink, and where the dead bodies are, there is he to be seen.

Will he who is protesting give teaching to the Ruler of all? Let him who has arguments to put forward against God give an answer. (Job.38.1-40.1 BBE)

THIRD SECRET

SNOWY DAY IS THE STORY OF POSSIBILITY OF SWIFT, IMMEDIATE AND LIFE-TRANSFORMING CHANGE

*- God's power of instant and complete
change and turnarounds*

Snow is a wonderful spectacle. Before it comes, you can see your house, landscape, etc. but when it begins to fall, the entire landscape, the whole place is transformed into whiteness. Houses, cars, vehicles, streets, everything is blanketed suddenly with a blanket of whiteness. You can travel but when you return to meet snow, you would hardly know your way again. For everything would have become one continuous sheet of whiteness. And the incredible change in landscape and environment can occur in minutes! Lush green landscape can become all velvety white in minutes. Dirty, scrappy neighborhood can become all invitingly white in minutes! Barren, desolate, unkempt land can become all fluffy white in minutes!

That speaks of the power of God to transform situations in the twinkle of an eye. In the season of the Arab awakening, we saw governments that have lasted 30, 40 years, led by strong-men, dictators and leaders, governments assumed to be invincible, all falling like dominos. Those governments and leaders were overthrown one after another in matter of months!

Joseph was a slave and prisoner in ancient Egypt but when the time for his release and unveiling came, he was released from prisoner and appointed to prime minister of Egypt all within hours! Check out Genesis 41. Joseph experienced the snowfall type of God's transformation powers! For someone reading this, it is tine for your transformation to come like snowfall – suddenly, quickly and all encompassing!

Transformation Comes
When I see the snow, I know that my transformation is on the way. In 2 Kings 6:24-30, there was siege against a city - famine situation of the people of the city of Samaria was so bad that they were eating their children. But a man of God came and declared that change was on the way! And the whole situation – long lasting, terrible beyond words – yet was transformed in one day, and the siege was lifted. But the one person who doubted the ability for change and transformation to occur in 24 hours died, seeing but not enjoying the transformation. Read the incredible story for yourself and dare to believe God for snow-type speedy transformation:

> *Now after this, Ben- hadad, king of Aram, got together*
> *all his army and went up to make an attack on Samaria,*

shutting the town in on all sides with his forces. And they became very short of food in Samaria; for they kept it shut in till the price of an ass's head was eighty shekels of silver, and a small measure of doves 'droppings was five shekels of silver.

And when the king of Israel was going by on the wall, a woman came crying out to him, and said, Help! my lord king. And he said, If the Lord does not give you help, where am I to get help for you? from the grain- floor or the grape- crusher? And the king said to her, What is troubling you? And she said in answer, This woman said to me, Give your son to be our food today, and we will have my son tomorrow. So, boiling my son, we had a meal of him; and on the day after I said to her, Now give your son for our food; but she has put her son in a secret place.

Then the king, hearing what the woman said, took his robes in his hands, violently parting them; and, while he was walking on the wall, the people, looking, saw that under his robe he had haircloth on his flesh. Then he said, May God's punishment come on me if Elisha, the son of Shaphat, keeps his head on his body after this day. But Elisha was in his house, and the responsible men were seated there with him; and before the king got there, Elisha said to those who were with him, Do you see how this cruel and violent man has sent to take away my life? While he was still talking to them, the king came down and said, This evil is from the Lord; why am I to go on waiting any longer for the Lord?

Then Elisha said, Give ear to the word of the Lord: the Lord says, Tomorrow, about this time, a measure of good meal will be offered for the price of a shekel and two measures of barley for a shekel, in the market- place of Samaria.

Then the captain whose arm was supporting the king said to the man of God, Even if the Lord made windows in heaven, would such a thing be possible? And he said, Your eyes will see it, but you will not have a taste of the food.

Now there were four lepers seated at the doorway into the town: and they said to one another, Why are we waiting here for death? If we say, We will go into the town, there is no food in the town, and we will come to our end there; and if we go on waiting here, death will come to us. Come then, let us give ourselves up to the army of Aram: if they let us go on living, then life will be ours; and if they put us to death, then death will be ours. So in the half light they got up to go to the tents of Aram; but when they came to the outer line of tents, there was no one there.

For the Lord had made the sound of carriages and horses, and the noise of a great army, come to the ears of the Aramaeans, so that they said to one another, Truly, the king of Israel has got the kings of the Hittites and of the Egyptians for a price to make an attack on us. So they got up and went in flight, in the half light, without their tents or their horses or their asses or any of their goods; they went in flight, fearing for their lives.

And when those lepers came to the outer line of tents, they went into one tent, and had food and drink, and took from it silver and gold and clothing, which they put in a secret place; then they came back and went into another tent from which they took more goods, which they put away in a secret place.

Then they said to one another, We are not doing right. Today is a day of good news, and we say nothing: if we go on waiting here till the morning, punishment will come to us. So let us go and give the news to those of the king's house. So they came in, and, crying out to the door- keepers of the town, they gave them the news, saying, We came to the tents of the Aramaeans, and there was no one there and no voice of man, only the horses and the asses in their places, and the tents as they were.

Then the door- keepers, crying out, gave the news to those inside the king's house. Then the king got up in the night and said to his servants, This is my idea of what the Aramaeans have done to us. They have knowledge that we are without food; and so they have gone out of their tents, and are waiting secretly in the open country, saying, When they come out of the town, we will take them living and get into the town. And one of his servants said in answer, Send men and let them take five of the horses which we still have in the town; if they keep their lives they will be the same as those of Israel who are still living here; if they come to their death they will be the same as all those of Israel who have gone to destruction: let us send and see.

So they took two horsemen; and the king sent them after the army of the Aramaeans, saying, Go and see. And they went after them as far as Jordan; and all the road was covered with clothing and vessels dropped by the Aramaeans in their flight. So those who were sent went back and gave the news to the king. Then the people went out and took the goods from the tents of the Aramaeans.

So a measure of good meal was to be had for the price of a shekel, and two measures of barley for a shekel, as the Lord had said. And the king gave authority to that captain, on whose arm he was supported, to have control over the doorway into the town; but he was crushed to death there under the feet of the people, as the man of God had said when the king went down to him.

So the words of the man of God came true, which he said to the king: Two measures of barley will be offered for the price of a shekel and a measure of good meal for a shekel, tomorrow about this time in the market- place of Samaria. And that captain said to the man of God, Even if the Lord made windows in heaven, would such a thing be possible? And he said to him, Your eyes will see it, but you will not have a taste of the food. And such was his fate; for he was crushed to death under the feet of the people, in the doorway into the town. (2Kings 6.24-7.20 BEB)

Swift and Sudden Change

Snow is a reflection and physical confirmation of God's power and ability of sudden, overwhelming and complete change, turnaround and transformation. One minute you see the whole landscape dry and quiet. Then snow comes suddenly and within an hour, you can't believe it is the same place you are seeing – it has become all white, snowy and velvety snow white! What a glorious transformation!

We saw how Joseph became prime minister in one day from being prisoner- moving from a slave to prime minister! The fact that snow came after so many years of glorious warming, is a confirmation that God's word never fails. It also shows that we will be remembered.

So when you see the snow, you see confirmation of God's power in your life to work quick change and transformation. **His word will come to pass in your life this very year, this very winter season! Before this winter runs out, someone reading this will be transformed like Joseph!**

God's transformation power does not happen once: it happens time and again. In my life, in a very short period of time, so many things happened in quick succession: I got supernatural, progressive changes in my business, career, ministry, home, on all fronts. Everything that had been confused, not working and stagnant, suddenly fell in place within a space of time – what God alone could do! May the Lord cause things to fall into place for you, in your favour this season.

FOURTH SECRET

SNOWY DAY IS THE STORY OF SNOW WHITE WASH!

– God's power to save!

Come now, and let us reason together, saith the LORD: though your sins be as scarlet, they shall be as white as snow; though they be red like crimson, they shall be as wool (Isaiah 1:18).

The snow is vivid physical illustration of the power of God to save, deliver and to transform lives. The worst part of any city will look very different and be transformed physically when blanketed by snow. If you were to go an unsavoury area of any major city in Europe, you could see signs of neglect or dereliction, Normally, you will not feel attracted to go there, but if you go there when the snow has fallen, you could never imagine that that place is the same terrible place you once knew. All dereliction and neglect will be all gone and hidden. Instead, all you see is an incredible area all white and glorious. For the period of snowfall, the dereliction disappears, covered by snowfall!

The snowy day is pure physical testimony and confirmation of the God's saving power. There is no life too low, too bad, too terrible that cannot be transformed, saved and redeemed at the cross of Calvary. There is no life too dark that cannot be by covered and blanketed permanently by the wonder-cleansing blood of Jesus.

I have seen murderers, prostitutes, thieves, all types of those societies will 'lowest of the low' transformed through Jesus. It is both a great mystery and great wonder – how so thoroughly lives can be changed and transformed through encounters with Jesus.Society will do well to return to God for right and proper behavior to be taught to all.

Top Actor Kirk Cameron's Testimony: Growing Pains
*Kirk Cameron, former star of Growing Pains, had everything most people want – fame, money, looks, and success. None of that compared to the joy he later found in knowing Christ, being forgiven, and being in a right relationship with God. Kirk explains how, as a young actor, he visited a church and heard the gospel for the very first time – and how Jesus revolutionized every aspect of his life. **http://www.washedred.com***

Raul Ries's Testimony: From Fury to Freedom
Raul's difficult childhood led him to be violent, angry and abusive towards his family. He had planned to kill his wife and

kids one day until he accidently turned on a television with his gun and heard about Jesus' forgiveness. He turned from his evil desires and began hating his sin. Read more on **www.washedred.com**.

Corrie Ten Boom's Testimony: The Hiding Place
A brave Dutch woman named Corrie ten Boom shares her amazing story about her imprisonment during the Holocaust in World War II and how she was able to help hundreds of people escape death. Read her incredible first hand report on **www.washred.com**.

Jason's Testimony: Freedom from Homosexuality
Jason lived a homosexual lifestyle for many years since he was a young child. It was not until God saved him that he was delivered from his evil desires and began hating his homosexuality and was changed to right living. Read and hear directly on **www.washedred.com**.

Nicky Cruz's Testimony: Gang Leader Miracle
Nicky was a violent New York City street gang leader and then his life was miraculously transformed by Jesus Christ. Hear the amazing story of Nicky Cruz on **www.washedred.com**

Richard Wurmbrand's Testimony: The Beauty of Nothing
Richard Wurmbrand was put in jail for 14 years because of his faith in Jesus Christ, but experienced joy and peace even though he was tortured and had no possessions. Read his story first-hand on www.washedred.com.

Sean Demars' Testimony: He Showed Me the Depths of My Sin

Sean Demars grew up being abused by an alcoholic and drug addicted mother. He became angry at God, incarcerated, institutionalized, and addicted to drugs. He thought there was no hope until Jesus showed him the depths of his sin. Read first hand on **www.washedred.com**.

Russell Mathis's Testimony: Breaking the Bonds of Pornography

The lure of pornography took hold of Russell's life like a deadly cancer until Jesus Christ delivered him from this dangerous addiction. Read the exciting story firsthand on **www.washred.com**.

Michael's Testimony: Atheist Saved by the Truth

Michael was challenged with the true Truth while on a college campus and he soon came to realize that his philosophy and atheism could not stand against the power of the Gospel. Read Michael's story on **www.washedred.com**.

Tim Conway's Testimony: Filled with God's Grace

Tim Conway was a crazy guy living the beer commercial lifestyle. Depression and emptiness eventually overtook his life until he experienced the grace of God. Read all on **www.washred.com**.

Ozzy's Testimony: I Called Upon The Lord

Ozzy grew up in Christian home and tried doing good things as he grew up. But, he living a sinful lifestyle and had no peace until he heard the true gospel and believed in Christ. Read all on *www.washred.com*.

Sharron's Testimony: Seeking Answers
Sharron was looking for something more in life than parties and friends. She started seeking the Bible for answers and found what she was missing all along. Read more on *www.washred.com*.

The Charles "Tex" Watson's Story: Forgiven
Former star athlete Charles "Tex" Watson was headed for greatness, but his feelings of emptiness led him into following Charles Manson and eventually getting into drug abuse and murder. Then he found God's mercy and his life turned around. Read about his turn around on *www.washed.com*.

Jon Courson's Testimony: Triumph through Tragedy
After the death of his wife and daughter in separate car accidents, hear the fascinating story of how Jon Courson found peace that only God can provide in our most difficult times. Read and hear his firsthand story on *www.washred.com*.

Nicole Richie's Testimony: A Restless Conscience
Nicole Richie was a youth singer in the worship band, and went to church for the fellowship with friends. Sadly she only knew religion and not Christ and was not born. Then her life was turn around when she met Jesus. Read her story firsthand on *www.washred.com*.

Julie's Story: Good Enough for Heaven?
Julie expected to go to Heaven since she was a good person until she realized that wasn't good enough. Read her firsthand report on www.washred.com.

A Committed Marxist Discovers Jesus Christ
Gerald Daly, who became the administrator for Allen Hall, the Westminster diocesan seminary, was for many years an atheist and committed Marxist. Check out Gerald's his faith story and how Jesus Christ came to him and transformed his life http://www.ccr.org.uk/testimon.htm.

Freedom in Christ
Vijaykumar Rajah, who was a drug addict for many years, shares his testimony and how he found Christ in Cardiff prison and the difference his new found faith has made to his life. Check out http://www.ccr.org.uk/testimon.htm.

Michela's Story
A young woman, who left her marriage for a violent abuser, shares however much you mess up your life, it's never too late to come back to Christ and he will help you.

Jesus – the Master of master turn-arounds
Even when we have made mistakes, if we go to God, He washes us no matter how dirty we are. I met a man years ago, who told me that he has killed several people, and it keeps tormenting him every day, and could not believe that God could ever forgive him. God does not want us to remain in our sinful state. The snow is a representation

of God's mercy: through it, God is saying to you, that if you come to Him, He will wash you and put away that trouble.

If we confess our sins, he is faithful and just to forgive us our sins, and to cleanse us from all unrighteousness (1 John 1:9). The bible says that anyone who hides his sins will not prosper.

Are there issues you need to bring before the Lord? Go ahead and tell Him today. Do not be like those who will come in their filthy state and return the same way. Are you right with the Lord?

Do you want more out of life – then you are a candidate for life surgery! Is life for run like Groundhog day – never ending cycle of monotony?

Your Invitation
Purge me with hyssop, and I shall be clean: wash me, and I shall be whiter than snow. Ps 51.7

Come now, and let us reason together, saith the LORD: though your sins be as scarlet, they shall be as white as snow; though they be red like crimson, they shall be as wool. Is 1.18.

FIFTH SECRET

THE SNOWY DAY IS PARABLE AND PHYSICAL GLIMPSE OF HEAVENLY CLOTHING AND GLORY

I beheld till the thrones were cast down, and the Ancient of days did sit, whose garment was white as snow, and the hair of his head like the pure wool: his throne was like the fiery flame, and his wheels as burning fire. (Dan 7.9)

Glimpse of Heavenly Raiment

We learn another secret from the snow on a snowy day. The snow is so fluffy and comfortable. It is like a teddy bear. The whiteness is so sparkling. There is a glory surrounding the snow, particularly when you go to the mountaintop; it is so unique and beautiful. It becomes even more glistening when the bright sunlight shines upon the snow-clad landscape – that is such an awesome spectacle.

That glorious whiteness is perhaps the nearest the
physical eyes will ever behold the glory of Heaven. So
when you see the glorious pure whiteness of the full
snowy day, you are getting a glimpse of the glory of
heaven.

> *And his raiment became shining, exceeding white as
> snow; so as no fuller on earth can white them (Mark
> 9:3).*

> *I beheld till the thrones were cast down, and the
> Ancient of days did sit, whose garment was white as
> snow, and the hair of his head like the pure wool: his
> throne was like the fiery flame, and his wheel as
> burning fire (Daniel 7:9).*

What does God's garment look like? It is as white as
snow. When you see the glory of the snow, God is giving
us the briefest glimpse of what His glory looks like. Yet
the glorious sparkle of bright sun shining on snow-clad
landscape is still yet a poor reflection of Heaven. The
snow is a glimpse but a very poor copy of the glory of
Heaven. I look forward eagerly to the glorious original in
Heaven. I pray that you the reader will make Heaven to
see the glory prepared by Jesus for His sons and
daughters. Please plan to make it to heaven!

Facial Reflection of Glory
Moses asked God to show him His glory, but at the end of
the long conversation, Moses saw only His back. At

another time when Moses went to the mountain and spent some time with the Lord, by the time he came down, the people could not behold his face, because God's glory had rubbed off on his face. The glory of God reflected on Moses' face and countenance was so sparkling that others could not stand such radiance and Moses had to use a veil for a season until his face became normal human again. The glory of God is dazzlingly sparkling.

> *And it came to pass, when Moses came down from mount Sinai with the two tables of the testimony in Moses' hand, when he came down from the mount, that Moses knew not that the skin of his face shone by reason of his speaking with him. And when Aaron and all the children of Israel saw Moses, behold, the skin of his face shone; and they were afraid to come nigh him. And Moses called unto them; and Aaron and all the rulers of the congregation returned unto him: and Moses spake to them. And afterward all the children of Israel came nigh: and he gave them in commandment all that Jehovah had spoken with him in mount Sinai. And when Moses had done speaking with them, he put a veil on his face. But when Moses went in before Jehovah to speak with him, he took the veil off, until he came out; and he came out, and spake unto the children of Israel that which he was commanded. And the children of Israel saw the face of Moses, that the skin of Moses' face shone: and Moses put the veil upon his face again, until he went in to speak with him. Ex 34.29-35*

Snow glimpses of Heaven

Martin Luther defined marriage as God's best way of explaining Himself. To me, the snowy day is the nearest best way to physically describe what the whiteness glory of Heaven looks like.

> *His countenance was like lightning, and his raiment*
> *white as snow: (Matt 28.3).*

When Jesus was transformed on the mount of Transfiguration, His dress became as white as snow. The glory of God's garment is so white that even the snow you can see is far from being truly white compared to the whiteness of Heavenly raiment. Yet, the Snow is the nearest the physical senses can comprehend the physical glory of God and the raiment of Heaven. In Revelation 1:12-18, we see the descriptions of the glory of God, which John saw.

> *And turning to see the voice which said these words to*
> *me, I saw seven gold vessels with lights burning in*
> *them; And in the middle of them one like a son of man,*
> *clothed with a robe down to his feet, and with a band*
> *of gold round his breasts. And his head and his hair*
> *were white like wool, as white as snow; and his eyes*
> *were as a flame of fire; And his feet like polished brass,*
> *as if it had been burned in a fire; and his voice was as*
> *the sound of great waters. And he had in his right hand*
> *seven stars: and out of his mouth came a sharp two-*
> *edged sword: and his face was like the sun shining in*

its strength. And when I saw him, I went down on my face at his feet as one dead. And he put his right hand on me, saying, Have no fear; I am the first and the last and the Living one; And I was dead, and see, I am living for ever, and I have the keys of death and of Hell. Rev 1.12-18 BBE

Handel's Hallelujah – the man who caught a Glimpse of Heaven

The oratorio – Hallelujah Chorus – is so spectacular and so vividly describes the glory of Court of Heaven that it conveys the overwhelming glory of Court of Heaven expressed in music sand drama. From the moment I first Heard the oratorio, I concluded that Handel must have caught a glimpse of Heaven when he wrote the chorus. The fullness of the story! Indeed he saw the court of heaven and that is what he tried to describe in the Oratorio!

Steve Gray's account of Handel's "Halleluyah Chorus – the rest of the story":

In a small London house on Brook Street, a servant arranges a tray full of food. For more than a week, he has faithfully continued to wait on his employer, an eccentric composer, who spends hour after hour isolated in his own room. morning, noon, and evening the servant delivers meals to the composer and returns later to find the food untouched.

Once again, he forces himself to go through the same

routine, complaining under his breath about the strange behavior of musicians. As he swings open the door to the composer's room, the servant stops in his tracks.

The startled composer, tears streaming down his face, turns to his servant and cries out, **"I did think I did see all Heaven before me, and the great God Himself."** *George Frederic Handel had just finished writing a movement that would take its place in history as the Hallelujah Chorus.*

Although Handel wrote his greatest music in England , he suffered personal setbacks there as well. He fell in and out of favor with changing governments, competing with established English composers, and dealing with hard-to-please audiences he found himself bankrupt.

Audiences for Handel's music were unpredictable, and the Church of England attacked him for what they considered his practice of writing biblical music to be performed in secular theaters. Handel drove himself to recover from one failure after another, and finally his health began to fail. By 1741 he was swimming in debt. It seemed certain he would land in debtor's prison.

On April 8 of that year, he gave what he considered his farewell concert. Miserably discouraged, he felt forced to retire from public activities at the age of fifty-six. Then two unforeseen events changed his life. A wealthy friend,

Charles Jensen, gave Handel a libretto based on the life of Christ, taken entirely from the bible. He also received a commission from Dublin charity to compose work for a benefit performance.

Handel set to work composing on August 22 in his little house on Brook Street in London. He grew so absorbed in the work that he rarely left his room, hardly stopping to eat. Within six days part one was complete. In nine days more he had finished part two, and in another six, part three. In all 260 pages of manuscript were filled in the remarkable short time of 24 days.

Messiah premiered on April 13, 1742 as a charitable benefit, raising 400 pounds and freeing 142 men from debtor's prison. A year later, Handel would perform his masterpiece in London. Controversy coming from the Church of England continued to plague Handel, yet the King of England attended the performance. As the first notes of the triumphant Hallelujah Chorus rang out, the king rose. Following the royal protocol, the entire audience stood too, initiating a tradition that has lasted more than two centuries.

The climax of this masterpiece is taken from Isaiah 40:5, "The glory of the LORD shall be revealed, And all flesh shall see *it together; For the mouth of the LORD has spoken.*"

SIXTH SECRET

SNOWY DAY - FLUFFY BUT ALSO DANGEROUS DAY - HANDLE WITH CARE!

The Snowy Day is parable and physical description of the loving but yet righteous character of God

And the cloud departed from off the tabernacle; and, behold, Miriam became leprous, white as snow: and Aaron looked upon Miriam, and, behold, she was leprous.(Nu 12.10)

The niceness, fluffiness and joyfulness of the snowy day

When the snow has fallen in its fullness, it creates a great day and atmosphere for play and joy. You ill find children playing in the snow, making snowmen, making ice-balls to throw at one another in joyful play. You will also find sledding and ice-skating if the snow is hard enough. Some extreme chaps will even skin-dive into wintry waters. In some cities, the main rivers become so hard that they become giant ice-skating rings. In one capital city, the hardened river become a car-racing track. Truly the snowy day is full of joy and excitement.

The difficulties, dangers and threats of the snowy day
Some snowy days become troublesome for some. When we had blizzards and the like schools, airports and work places are closed in reflection of the disruption and dangers of the snowy day. Some have been lef trapped outdoors by snow, stuck in cars and harsh terrain. Some have been left trapped in-doors unable to go source for doors for many days. Some have been trapped in-doors without warmth and heating. Many have died from the dangers of the snowy day

The niceness, fluffiness, joy and love of God and the dangerous God
Just as the snowy day has two sides, so is the character of God. One the one hand, God is pure love, loving, caring, always giving; He is a complete gentleman, never forcing Himself on any one. He made man in His own image with the power and liberty of choice. Yet He is a dangerous God. He only has the power and ability to destroy both physical and spiritual ife. He is the only one who can wipe out whole lives, nations and civilizations without trace. He is a great and good Lord but also a fearsome God.

The paradox of the snowy day – joyful, playful but danger'ful!
At snow time, with all the whiteness and fluffiness, we also hear and read about the troubles of the snowy day. On a snowy day, roads can be blocked, roads can become

impassable, lives can be lost, and many can be stranded. If proper preparation is not made well ahead for winter and snow, it is disastrous and in many cases life-threatening. Ahead of snowfall, the weather report is known and people are expected to prepare ahead. Any one who treats the snowy day with levity and carelessness will certainly get in deep trouble and may even lose his or her life.

The paradox of the Ancient of Days – Love and Righteousness

It is a great lesson that when dealing with the Lord, the Ancient of Days, you do not deal with Him casually or carelessly; likewise the snow. If you do not handle the snowy day with care, it will destroy. Hence we wear special warm clothing's, shoes with grip, and the house and habitation are kept warm, in extreme cases schools and work places are shut and people asked to stay home.

In the same way, the Holy One must be treated with greatest respect and care. Ending on the wrong side of God can mean death. Some people even in church l do not understand that trifling with the Almighty is death just as treating the snowy day with levity and carelessness can end in death. Hebrews 12 deserves careful reading.

For this reason, as we are circled by so great a cloud of witnesses, putting off every weight, and the sin into which we come so readily, let us keep on running in the way which is marked out for us, Having our eyes

*fixed on Jesus, the guide and end of our faith, who
went through the pains of the cross, not caring for the
shame, because of the joy which was before him, and
who has now taken his place at the right hand of God's
seat of power. Give thought to him who has undergone
so much of the hate of sinners against himself, so that
you may not be tired and feeble of purpose. Till now
you have not given your blood in your fight against
sin: And you have not kept in mind the word which
says to you as to sons, My son, do not make little of the
Lord's punishment, and do not give up hope when you
are judged by him; For the Lord sends punishment on
his loved ones; everyone whom he takes as his son has
experience of his rod.*

*It is for your training that you undergo these things;
God is acting to you as a father does to his sons; for
what son does not have punishment from his father?
But if you have not that punishment of which we all
have our part, then you are not true sons, but children
of shame. And again, if the fathers of our flesh gave us
punishment and had our respect, how much more will
we be under the authority of the Father of spirits, and
have life? For they truly gave us punishment for a
short time, as it seemed good to them; but he does it
for our profit, so that we may become holy as he is. At
the time all punishment seems to be pain and not joy:
but after, those who have been trained by it get from it
the peace- giving fruit of righteousness.*

For this cause let the hands which are hanging down be lifted up, and let the feeble knees be made strong, And make straight roads for your feet, so that the feeble may not be turned out of the way, but may be made strong. Let your desire be for peace with all men, and to be made holy, without which no man may see the Lord; Looking with care to see that no man among you in his behaviour comes short of the grace of God; for fear that some bitter root may come up to be a trouble to you, and that some of you may be made unclean by it; And that there may not be any evil liver, or any man without respect for God, like Esau, who let his birthright go for a plate of food. For you have knowledge that even long after, when he was desiring the blessing for his heritage, he was turned away, though he made his request frequently and with weeping; because the past might not be changed.

You have not come to a mountain which may be touched, and is burning with fire, and to a black cloud, and a dark smoke, and a violent wind, And to the sound of a horn, and the voice of words, the hearers of which made request that not a word more might be said to them: For the order which said, If the mountain is touched even by a beast, the beast is to be stoned, seemed hard to them; And the vision was so overpowering that even Moses said, I am shaking and full of fear.

But you have come to the mountain of Zion, to the place of the living God, to the Jerusalem which is in heaven, and to an army of angels which may not be numbered,

To the great meeting and church of the first of those who are named in heaven, and to God the judge of all, and to the spirits of good men made complete, And to Jesus by whom the new agreement has been made between God and man, and to the sign of the blood which says better things than Abel's blood.

See that you give ear to his voice which comes to you. For if those whose ears were shut to the voice which came to them on earth did not go free from punishment, what chance have we of going free if we give no attention to him whose voice comes from heaven? Whose voice was the cause of the shaking of the earth; but now he has made an oath, saying, There will be still one more shaking, not only of the earth, but of heaven.

And the words, Still one more, make it clear that there will be a taking away of those things which are shaking, as of things which are made, so that there may be only those things of which no shaking is possible. If then, we have a kingdom which will never be moved, let us have grace, so that we may give God such worship as is pleasing to him with fear and respect: For our God is an all- burning fire.

Where is God's honour?

In Malachi 1:6, God asked a very interesting question:

A son honoureth his father, and a servant his master: if then I be a father, where is mine honour? and if I be a master, where is my fear? saith the LORD of hosts unto

*you, O priests, that despise my name. And ye say,
Wherein have we despised thy name?*

Many honour their employers more than God. For fear of
losing their jobs, many go very early to work, but when it
comes to church, they go any time they like. We give more
gifts to the person we want to marry than to God who gave
the spouse to us. During Christmas, we buy and distribute
expensive gifts to our loved ones, but what do we give to
God? This is one of the secrets you will have to work with,
if you are going to go far with the Lord. Be careful to give
Him all the honour due Him.

The snowy day is a parable and warning not to trifle with
the Most High.

*And the cloud departed from off the tabernacle; and,
behold, Miriam became leprous, white as snow: and
Aaron looked upon Miriam, and, behold, she was
leprous. (Nu 12.10)*

*The leprosy therefore of Naaman shall cleave unto thee,
and unto thy seed for ever. And he went out from his
presence a leper as white as snow. (2kings 5.7)*

*When the Almighty scattered kings in it, it was white
as snow in Salmon. (Ps 68.14)*

SEVENTH SECRET

Snowy Day – The Uncomfortable season is also the season for exploits

The Snowy Day is parable of the opportunity for exploits waiting for people of exploits in the uncomfortable seasons of life

Benaiah the son of Jehoiada, the son of a valiant man of Kabzeel, who had done mighty deeds, he slew the two sons of Ariel of Moab: <u>he went down also and slew a lion in the midst of a pit in time of snow</u>. And he slew an Egyptian, a man of great stature, five cubits high; and in the Egyptian's hand was a spear like a weaver's beam; and he went down to him with a staff, and plucked the spear out of the Egyptian's hand, and slew him with his own spear. These things did Benaiah the son of Jehoiada, and had a name among the three mighty men. Behold, he was more honorable than the thirty, but he attained not to the first three: and David set him over his guard.1Chro 11.22-25

Benaiah was a key member of David's mighty and crazy gang and later army. David's men started with David when he was on exile running from King Saul. The men were the lowest of the low – in distress, in debt, without jobs, etc. but then they saw another man like them also in distress but with a solid future. Those men became perhaps the greatest army ever recorded.

> *And every one that was in distress, and every one that was in debt, and every one that was discontented, gathered themselves unto him; and he became captain over them: and there were with him about four hundred men. 1Sam 22.2*

All of David's men were exploit'ful. One of David's men was Benaiah. Benaiah left the comfort of shelter on a snowy day to confront a lion. He went out on a snowy day to fight with a lion. We know that on snowy days, most people would not want to leave their houses – rather you want to stay warm and well covered and sheltered. Among David's mighty men, Benaiah was not even the most spectacular yet he could still achieve in spite of the snow. He was among the second group of David's 30 mighty men. He was so brave and always ready to take up challenges and opportunities both in the comfortable and uncomfortable seasons of life. He was a man who was not comfortable to sit at home so long as there was a challenge to be taken up.

Even the snowy day is no detriment to a life of exploits.

EIGHT LESSONS FROM BENAIAH:

1. *He was a crazy man in a crazy group or gang.*
    When you are in the group of people who are going
    somewhere, you don't have much choice than to do
    the same. Because this man was in the group of the
    mighty, he became mighty. You need to watch the
    friends you keep; even the parable man says bad
    company corrupt good manners. But the strange
    thing is that all of them started as nonentities. They
    were people who were not going anywhere in life.
    They were the lowest people in the society, but they
    knew that young David who had killed giant Goliath
    had a call of God and a destiny in God, so they
    followed him even into exile, and while transforming
    David, God also transformed them. If you stick with
    a child of destiny, who is truly called of God and is
    obeying the Lord, your destiny will be impacted by
    his. It is a wise thing to stay with people who are
    going somewhere.

2. *He was bold and skillful.*
    He was a valiant man even though this was not the
    case at the beginning. This shows the need to put in
    your best in whatever you do. Why settle for less
    when you can be the best? It is extremely important to
    always put your best foot forward; if you will ever
    make an effort, let it be the one that cannot be denied
    the best of results. When David was going to fight
    Goliath, Saul gave him amour but he turned down

that offer and instead went with nothing else but the name of the Lord, a sling and some stones. He was not born skillful but he trained himself. This tells us that if you lack a particular skill, it does not mean that you cannot acquire it.

One way of knowing those who will make it in life, is by their readiness to learn what they do not know. How teachable are you? Today, some people are looking down on the skill that will give them their breakthrough. As long as they refuse to acquire what they need, they will turn their temporary bus stop into their final destination. In 1 Samuel 17, David became so skillful that only one skillful shot from his sling killed Goliath, and brought victory to his nation.

Benaiah was skillful because he learnt it from David. There are some things in our lives that look as if they are not important, but there are people who have become mighty through them. Years ago, I worked with a lawyer who had a cleaning business and it grew to become so big. One of our brothers works in the oil industry, but in his local church, he started a bookshop, and later, he and another sister opened another private business. Today, he has left the oil company and is now a prominent and prosperous bookseller, just because he took serious the little assignments given to him by the church. He told me he now makes millions from selling books. The bible says if you are not faithful in small things, you will not receive the big ones. See 1 Chronicles 12:1-3, 11-12, 14. This passage says the least of them was equal to 100 men, and the most powerful was equal to 1000 men. When we become skillful, we become people that our generation cannot understand. Pray that God should give you the power to become the best in whatever you do.

3. *Trustworthiness:* He was a man who was completely trust worthy to the call that God had given to him, as well as to others too. The first two verses tell us that some who came to join David were people from Saul's tribe; and David asked them if they had come to betray him. If you also consider verse 16 and 17, you will notice that to them, there were no divisive or tribal instincts, as their only desire was to do God's will. He was trustworthy even after the death of David. Many times, people start a journey but they wouldn't carry it on to the end.

4. *He was part of a non-static but ever increasing group of people.* All of them kept on increasing in strength, number, faith, doing exploits from one level to another. It is God's plan for us to increase positively. He does not want us to be stagnant. See 1 Chron. 12:22. Here, the bible described the army as the army of God. Stay with people who are increasing – in strength, babies, anointing, resources, etc.

5. *God was his focus: No sectional or tribal sentiment.* They all came for one purpose -to ensure that the word of God was established in Israel. They came to

David so that they could see God's word fulfilled (1 Chron. 12:23). Even those who were from Saul's tribe joined David to achieve the same purpose. No emotion or offense stood in their way. A man or woman who is going somewhere with God, wouldn't allow anything to hinder him or her. Such an individual would strive to do everything according to the word of God. There was a true story of one of the battalions of the Roman army. They were very close to Caesar to the extent that whenever they were given instructions, they obeyed promptly and completely. It was also said of that group that because they had received an instruction to stay in a particular location, even when danger surfaced later, they refused to leave, even though the logical thing would have been for them to run. How committed are you to God?

Check out 2 Sam 23:20; 1 Cor. 11.
The men who were gathered with David became great people. Yet when they started off, they were unknown, unimportant and very dispensable. What took them from their lowly place into a place of greatness? In 1 Samuel 22:1-2, you see the story of how they were when they started off. Economic distress is a fact throughout history - they were distressed, debtors and discontented fellows. There is an organization called CAP which is an acronym for Christians Against Poverty. How did it come about? Its founder was a banker who encountered so many problems until he became heavily indebted, and he called

upon God, and God delivered him. Thereafter, he decided to teach others how to manage their resources, including how to get out of debts. In other words, God can help you to turn a nagging problem into the solution you have always craved for. God wants us not just to be free from distress, debts and other problems, but also to lift our generation. In 1 Chron.11:22 and 2 Sam. 19, their lives changed and they became mighty men. Benaiah did something smart – he saw people who were going somewhere and joined them. If a man stays with people who are not going anywhere, over time, he will be like them.

An older man who was not a lawyer told me the story of two people who started practicing law in his home city - one loved parties and the drinking lifestyle, while the other did not. While the former latter will be returning from a party, the former would be studying; and forty years later, the diligent fellow had become a prominent lawyer. Get yourself around people who are going places. Let us train ourselves in all that we do. If you want to be a cook, be the best cook.

6. *Another virtue in Benaiah was commitment.* The issue of commitment is so vital in the church today. Commitment is so important that Jesus had to ask the disciples in John 6:7 whether they wanted to leave Him like others did. Benaiah was so skillful that he displaced a man of his sword and used it to kill him. We need to become skillful in whatever we do. He

was thoroughly committed to the assignment, to David, and everything David stood for.

One thing that God cannot handle is lack of commitment. When He taught what was considered a hard doctrine, many of Jesus' followers began to leave, but when He asked if the disciples were also leaving, they said they were going nowhere. We need to work on our level of commitment – to God, His service and our relationships. Those who left Jesus were not there on the day of Pentecost. They were not there when Jesus resurrected, when Paul joined the church, when Holy Spirit came down, when ordinary men began to preach and extraordinary miracles began to happen, etc. they lost out just because they were not committed. Recently, I was reading a story about India: the statistics showed that almost all marriages in India were arranged, yet the divorce rate was only one percent. Why? It is because they are committed whereas in the church it is not so. God's perfect desire is that we should be stable. Elijah had the same problem when Jezebel threatened him with death. As far as I am concerned, divorce is not an option to marriage. When David started off, it was just David and his brothers and Benaiah joined them. The bible says that group grew so big that it was comparable to the army of God. (1 Chron. 12:22). Why? They kept on increasing, in numbers, skills, commitment, resources, knowledge and more. From now on, you too can begin to increase in love, resources, wisdom, wealth, grace, fruit of the womb, etc.

7. *They were unreasonable people.*
    The world cannot be changed by reasonable people.
    Reasonable people adapt to the philosophies of the
    world, while unreasonable people insist that the
    world should change to be like them.   If you are
    reasonable as a Christian, you cannot be what God
    wants you to be. Romans 8:19 says the whole of
    creation is waiting for the manifestation of the sons
    and daughters of God, and we cannot manifest if we
    are reasonable people. You would be amazed to
    know that the world is prospering through this
    principle. Some research work was carried out in a
    certain   part   of   England   some   time   ago.
    Questionnaires   were   executed   on   female   school
    pupils aged between 10 and 13 years. The pupils were
    asked what they would like to become when they
    grow up – the more frequent answer was to become
    footballers' wives! Since when did marrying a
    footballer become a career or profession? They didn't
    say they wanted to become doctors, nurses, singers,
    actors, models, or the like. As we speak, there is no
    course in any college or university where one can
    study to become a footballer's wife. How could such
    children grow up with such a mindset if not in
    response to the way the media and society project
    such as an ideal image? It for our own good to
    become people of exploits, so that we can affect or
    change society rather than conform to a value-
    deficient society that is taking society nowhere.

8. *Benaiah left his house on a snowy day* to go and confront the lion that was out there terrorizing the people of his day. That lion represents whatever is challenging our generation. If challenges come to you, ask God for direction on how to face them. I have discovered that whatever troubles you the most is most likely an assignment that God wants to give. What troubled Joseph the most were his dreams: they attracted the envy of his brothers which made them to sell him into slavery. Yet, it was still the same dreams that made him what he was. The world famous Guinness Book of Records came into being through certain challenging situations. It all began when one of the managing directors of Guinness book of record, who was a king fisherman and golfer would go fishing or golfing with colleagues and there would be unresolved arguments over the result. So each time they went to fish and somebody caught a big fish, they would begin to debate on whether it was the biggest or not, and so were there controversies in gulfing. It troubled the man so much that when he had some money, he commissioned someone to put it into record so that there would be no more arguments for such. But today, it has gone beyond a few individuals and is now covering the whole world, and they are now making money through it. That was how the book came into being. So each time there was an argument, the details were documented. Always remember to share what troubles you with God because He has your destiny in His hands and He is

willing to help you.

Moreover, as earlier stated, God was his focus: He had no tribal or other selfish interests (1Sam. 25:28-31). What they were conscious about was how to help David actualize his dream. Their focus was to run the race that they saw David running. If you truly want to run the race, you must be focused giving no room for sentiment. Abigail told David that he should not bother himself with her foolish husband because it could divert his attention from where he was going. Then she asked David to remember her when he gets to his destination, and that was why David quickly married her when her husband died; he saw her as a smart and spiritual woman. Our assignment is to turn our world upside down.

At the end, Benaiah and his groups became people of exploits- 2 Sam. 23:20-39. That is why they could be referred to as the snowy day crew – people that did what their generation could not do in spite of their limitations. What are the limitations confronting you today? What are the reasons for not advancing or achieving those noble goals and programmes? If Benaiah and his men could achieve great goals for their nation, you too can do exploits for your nation, and particularly for God's kingdom. Make the right move today and the Lord will back you up.

EIGHTH SECRET

EVERYTHING MADE BY GOD HAS A DIVINE PURPOSE AND IS WORTH CELEBRATING

For he saith to the snow, Fall thou on the earth; Likewise to the shower of rain, And to the showers of his mighty rain. Job 37.6

Hast thou entered the treasuries of the snow, Or hast thou seen the treasures of the hail, 23 Which I have reserved against the time of trouble, Against the day of battle and war? Job 8.22-23

The snow was created by God with a particular quality, character and purpose. It may look meaningless to men but the snow was specially made for special purposes. As with the snow so is everything created by Heaven! Every creature and creation has a purpose and meaning. Inanimate objects and substances and animate creatures all have function, purpose and meaning. The creatures are the handiwork of a Great God. Nothing was made without purpose, meaning or name. Since He alone understand the fullness of His creations, God loves to celebrate all He made.

The biggest as well as the smallest creatures each have their own glory and purpose – all created by Heaven. There is nothing made that is completely void of purpose, beauty or function. The Lord celebrates the regality of the Lion as well as the wisdom of the ants:

> *There are four things which are little upon the earth, But they are exceeding wise: The ants are a people not strong, Yet they provide their food in the summer; The conies are but a feeble folk, Yet make they their houses in the rocks; The locusts have no king, Yet go they forth all of them by bands; The lizard taketh hold with her hands, Yet is she in kings 'palaces. There are three things which are stately in their march, Yea, four which are stately in going: The lion, which is mightiest among beasts, And turneth not away for any; The greyhound; The he- goat also; And the king against whom there is no rising up. Prov 30.24-31*

So we see that everything and everyone was created for a specific purpose, function and assignment. Since you are made in God's personal image, you are created, destined and expected to impact your generation! God celebrates you because of the great potential of greatness written into your DNA.

For you formed my inmost being. You knit me together in my mother's womb. I will give thanks to you, For I am fearfully and wonderfully made. Your works are wonderful. My soul knows that very well. My frame wasn't hidden from you, When I was made in secret, Woven together in the depths of the earth. Your eyes saw my body. In your book they were all written, The days that were ordained for me, When as yet there were none of them. How precious to me are your thoughts, God! How vast is the sum of them! If I would count them, they are more in number than the sand. When I wake up, I am still with you. Ps139.13-18 ASV

Question is when will you begin to walk, demonstrate and live in the greatness written in your DNA – written into your DNA by Heaven?

For the strong desire of every living thing is waiting for the revelation of the sons of God. Ro 8.19

BOOK TWO

THE BLESSINGS AND INSPIRATIONS OF THE SNOWY DAY

AND STORY OF BENAIAH AND THE SNOWY DAY CREW

Journey into the great storehouses of heaven and your blessings

The winter of late 2009 into early 2010 in Europe has been said to be the coldest and most sustained snow season in about thirty years. The winter of 2010 into 2011 proved to be even colder and harsher. Roads were closed, many towns and villages were not reachable, many accidents, airports closed, travel turmoil, rural areas running out of oils and other supplies, deaths and total mayhem. The abundance of snow had overwhelmed the ability of many local councils to clear up the snow, while supplies of salt to grit roads to make them safer became scarce. Many see the snow as troublesome and altogether a very bad experience. However, I bring you great news, another perspective and great tidings of a different type!

Wintery snow fulfils scripture as everything falls into place. If you were in Scotland in the winter of 2009-2010, you would have experienced the coldest and longest sustained winter in Europe in about 30 years. That is so great and exhilarating! Therefore, we are more confident that more seasons of our lives will be remembered.

PROLOGUE

The winter of late 2009 and early 2010 in Scotland, the United Kingdom and Europe in general was a winter that would be remembered, a winter that would enter into the annals of history. It was said to be the coldest winter and most sustained snowfall in in the United Kingdom and Europe in some thirty years . Uncharacteristically in view of the previous couple of years, much of the United Kingdom, North and middle Europe experienced a 'White Christmas' and a 'white' new year.

CHAPTER 1

A SNOWY SEASON TO REMEMBER

In ancient times, there was a teenager, growing up with his many brothers and parents. He had visions and thoughts of himself and his future. He would dream that he was to become a great leader. Other times, he would see himself becoming so great that he would become head over all his family including his parents and his older brothers. One night, he had an audacious dream, in which he saw himself ruling over the moon and stars. Being the teenager that he was, he was so excited about his dreams of greatness such that he told everybody around him. He ended up exasperating everyone with the constant recounting of his dreams of coming greatness. His father and brothers were upset and began to call him 'the dreamer' in a sarcastic and belittling way. His brothers were increasingly irritated by their youngest brother who was also their father's favourite.

One day, while the brothers were in the fields looking after their father's flocks, they saw the teenager coming in a distance and they starting talking about their brother, the dreamer. The talk led to something more sinister as one of the brothers suggested that they should get rid of him once and for all, to put an end to his talk of future greatness and grandeur.

Slightly wiser counsel prevailed that it was not proper to kill their own brother. Instead, his big brothers sold him into slavery; to a band of slave traders who were passing by. This young teenage dreamer left the comfort of his father's house and love and was sold into the terrible life of slavery in a foreign land. The dreamer became a slave. What would become of his dreams?

Over the next 13 years, he was a slave in the house of a leading official in the city where he was taken. The city was also the capital of the ancient Egyptian Empire ruled by the Pharaohs. Even though a slave, the teenage dreamer turned young man was very industrious and competent, so much so that he soon became housekeeper in that household. He rose to become the butler of the household; however, trouble was not far away. The woman of the house soon became fascinated with the young dreamer and wanted to have an affair with him. He refused to go that way, and eventually her anger at being rebuffed led her to falsely accuse him of attempted rape. The accusation led to him being sent him to prison. The young dreamer descended from slavery to prisoner. What would become of his dreams?

Even in prison, his industriousness and diligence shone once more and he became the 'top' prisoner. In addition to working hard, he cared for people and was always looking for ways to help others. By this time, he had become proficient at interpreting dreams. He used his gift and skill of interpretation of dreams to help two key fellow prisoners, who had had perplexing dreams. In ancient times, even more than today, kings and ordinary citizens alike depended on magicians, fortune-tellers and witch doctors to guide them with their spiritual insight. The young dreamer continued doing very well in jail, to the extent, you can describe life in prison as such. Elsewhere and in the great palace of Pharaoh to be precise, the king had a dream one night that troubled him greatly. He woke up and summoned all his magicians and astrologers and told them his dream, asking them to interpret it, but they could not. Pharaoh was very perplexed until one of his officials who had encountered the young dreamer in prison, and who had once had his own dream interpreted by the young dreamer slave prisoner. The high official recalled the ability of the young dreamer slaver prisoner and told Pharaoh about the young man. So began the most amazing day and night in the life of the young dreamer. He was rushed out of prison, shaved, had his clothes changed and ushered into audience with Pharaoh. Pharaoh recounted his troubling dream and the young dreamer accurately interpreted pharaoh's dream. The dream described the boom that was coming to the nation which was to be followed by a season of bust and economic downturn. He then proceeded to give Pharaoh sound strategic advice on how to carefully use the season of boom to prepare for the season of bust.

Pharaoh was so pleased and excited at the interpretation as well as strategic counsel for what to do that he immediately appointed the young man as his Prime Minister. His responsibility was to prepare the country during the season of boom for the famine that was to come during the following season of bust. That day and night became a day and night that the young dreamer would always remember with awe and amazement that he was transformed from being a slave and prisoner to being the Prime Minister in one day. His story became history and a legendary note.

Joseph the young dreamer had experienced the season when God transforms a man or woman suddenly. One week the person appears to be without hope and without a future, the next, he has shot to the top! There are particular seasons in the lives of God's people when they get so transformed that it is beyond belief. Personally, I remember one year that was pivotal in my life - everything was transformed for me. That year, the Lord relocated me, gave me a great promotion in my career, a transforming position, helped me start of a new level of ministry and led me to my wife. It is a year that I will always remember. In our church, we will remember the year in which the Lord handed us an old church building worth over a million pounds (two million dollars). It is a year to be remembered.

For someone reading this, I prophesy that you are entering your own memorable season and year, a time that will be packed with transformations and breakthroughs ordained by the Lord. This season and year will become one that you will always be remembered. The winter of 2009/2010, the coldest winter in 30 years, had the most sustained snowfall in 30 years and became for us a confirmation that we have entered a season that will be remembered for good and miraculous transformation. Enter into your own memorable season

Points to Remember and Pray:
There is a season, day, month or year that the Lord brings about an awesome, mind-boggling transformation in the life of a saint.

- Joseph experienced it. Genesis 41:1-16; 37-46
- Saul experienced it. He went simply to look for the family's lost donkeys. A simple journey turn out to be an incredible journey. Instead of returning with the lost donkeys, he returned as king over Israel. 1 Samuel 9-10:1
- Ruth experienced it when one morning Naomi, her mother-in-law, woke up her with a declaration that it was time for Ruth to get her own house and husband. Therefore started the quick succession of steps and events that ended with her becoming the wife to one of the most godly and eligible men in Israel. Ruth 3:1-6; 16-18

- Esther experienced it when from being just a young girl, an orphaned foreigner from a suspect nation; she became Queen over one of the greatest empire of ancient times. Esther 2:1-18

- Obama experienced it when in a breathtaking two years, he rose from near complete obscurity, from an 'wrong' colour and challenging background, he became senator and then the President of the United States of America.

- I have experienced many sweet and memorable seasons and years. Another such year is starting for us.

- What about you? Do you want to enter into your memorable season and year? Then ask the Incredible God for an incredible season to be opened to you.

- A lady completed her master's education and for two years could not secure any job. Her classmates all were progressing into careers but not so for her. She received so many regret letters including one from a leading global oil services company. Then she fell ill including long hospital stay. It looked like life was consistently going from worse to worse. Then between late November and early December of that year, in short space of time. Everything memorably turned round for good. Her health fully was restored. Then she got three job offers from three global leading companies and became nicely confused as to which one to accept. Of the three job offers, only one came from application and interview. The second was from one of the regrets a year earlier. The company changed its mind and invited her to start with them. The third was from a leading company that she did not even apply or interview for. The job offer from that company was thoroughly perplexing to her. How did they happen she asked the company representative? The response was that someone in the company who knew her in school recommended that she be offered a position that had become available. Strangely, she did not even recall the young man in question. But it was year in which God decided to make memorable for her. That was how she got an employment from a leading global company without applying or interviewing – what a memorable year!

- What about you? Do you want to enter into your memorable season and year? Then ask the Incredible God , the Lord of signs and wonders for an incredible season to be opened to you.

It is time to walk into your most memorable season.

Even the physical elements, the season of winter has become a winter (snow) season to be remembered. So everything is falling to us in pleasant places and even the weather pattern is confirming what we trust the Lord for.

A snowy day is a day that confirms that God would work absolute transformation in a day, in a month, in a year, in a season, in one life, one church, one city, one nation, one family, one tribe, one tongue. It is so exciting to see God's glory and power of instantaneous transformation written as a parable into the snowdy day and winter season.

[A Song of the going up.] When the Lord made a change in Zion's fate, we were like men in a dream. Then our mouths were full of laughing, and our tongues gave a glad cry; they said among the nations, The Lord has done great things for them. The Lord has done great things for us; because of which we are glad. Let our fate be changed, O Lord, like the streams in the South. Those who put in seed with weeping will get in the grain with cries of joy. Though a man may go out weeping, taking his vessel of seed with him; he will come again in joy, with the corded stems of grain in his arms. (Ps 126 BEB)

CHAPTER 2

A SNOWY DAY IS CONFIRMATION OF GOD'S FAITHFULNESS

Throughout the earth, the Lord has ordained seasons. In the tropics, there are two seasons: dry season and the wet or rainy season. In the northern hemisphere, we have four seasons: winter, spring, summer and autumn. However, in reality, there are two seasons: summertime and wintertime. The other two seasons are but transitions from summertime to wintertime and from wintertime to summertime.

Winter in the upper part of the Northern hemisphere is usually characterised by heavy snowfall and sub-zero temperatures. For many years before winters of 2009/2010, , the winters in Scotland and in the countries around the North Seas had become milder and un-extreme. In many years, snow fall was sparse and far from white Christmas scenes typically depicted on Christmas cards.

Then in the winters of 2009/2010, the heavens poured out tonnes and avalanches of snow. One gentleman I spoke with recalled that 1963 was the last winter he could recollect having such overabundance of snow and cold. The sparse snowfall in the winters preceding 2009/2010 had given more significance to the challenge of global warming and care (or mankind's lack of good care) of the Earth created by the Lord and handed to man for management.

> *While the earth remains, seedtime and harvest, and cold and heat, and summer and winter, and day and night shall not cease. (Gen 8:22 KJV)*

After living in Scotland and the North Sea area for many years, it seemed that snowfalls seem to decrease every winter until the winter of 2008/2009 when we saw the first significant increase of snowfall. In that winter we not only saw increased snowfall but also overwhelming snow showers and everything seem to have changed in a short time. What does this mean? It tells us that though men may be faithless; powerless to do the right thing; destructive to the environment; and not live to expectations, - God will always be faithful and will not fail us. He would keep his word concerning the earth and concerning you and me. That is why it is terrible and ultimately disastrous to trust in men instead of trusting God. At some point in time, putting your trust in a man or woman would fail.

Doom to those who go off to Egypt thinking that horses can help them, Impressed by military mathematics, awed by sheer numbers of chariots and riders — And to The Holy of Israel, not even a glance, not so much as a prayer to God. Still, he must be reckoned with, a most wise God who knows what he's doing. He can call down catastrophe. He's a God who does what he says. He intervenes in the work of those who do wrong, stands up against interfering evildoers. Egyptians are mortal, not God, and their horses are flesh, not Spirit. When God gives the signal, helpers and helped alike will fall in a heap and share the same dirt grave. This is what God told me:

"Like a lion, king of the beasts, that gnaws and chews and worries its prey, Not fazed in the least by a bunch of shepherds who arrive to chase it off, So God-of-the-Angel-Armies comes down to fight on Mount Zion, to make war from its heights. And like a huge eagle hovering in the sky, God-of-the-Angel-Armies protects Jerusalem. I'll protect and rescue it. Yes, I'll hover and deliver." (Isaiah 31:1-5 MSG)

Our God would always deliver on His promises. You should go to the Lord to discuss any promise concerning you that appears to be delayed or failing. Our God will always deliver and is always faithful. Snow falling is your confirmation that God would always deliver concerning his children. (See Isaiah 31:5b and Isaiah 30:18-26) Howbeit, ensure that you are in complete obedience (Isaiah 30:27-30).

When you see snow falling therefore that is your confirmation that God will never fail, but will always keep His word. The snowy day is your confirmation that the Lord keeps His promises.

> *While the earth remains, seedtime and harvest, and cold and heat, and summer and winter, and day and night shall not cease. (Gen 8:22 KJV)*

We have a responsibility to take good care of the earth, God's creation, which he handed to man through Adam. We also know that through and since Adam, man's destructive habits have been damaging to all of God's creation including man and God's earth. Global warming or not, God would keep His own promises - keeping His part of the bargain as long as the earth remains - summertime and wintertime will not cease. This gets me very excited. This knowledge gives me hope, great hope and confidence. This also gives me an added incentive to take responsibility to make right what God has given me, to manage His resources in my hands and under my influence correctly. To be faithful like He is, faithful to see and work for His Kingdom to populate the entire earth, faithful to be all He has ordained for me to become.
Will you do the same?

CHAPTER 3

SUDDENLY THE SNOW TRANSFORMED THE EARTH

S nowfall is a transformation and testament that change and transformation can come in the twinkling of an eye.

At a certain time, the earth, the terrain and the trees are all green and brown as they usually look. When it snows, it starts off looking like regular raindrops but when you look closer, you discover that the drops are bigger than the normal raindrops. You look closer still and see a flicker of white and you realise that it is actually snow!

In the northern hemisphere countries, snowfall is so looked forward to, particularly at Christmas, that the in the United Kingdom, the bookmakers take bets whether or not the coming Christmas would be a 'White Christmas'. The joy of Christmas is accentuated by the splendour of snow. It changes everything to a vibrant white splendour.

The snow starts of slowly and keeps falling and within a short space of time, everything and everywhere is transformed and covered in fluffy white - a white blanket of snow. Only our God can perform such a miracle that within minutes and hours the entire landscape is transformed - a feat that man can imitate but never achieve. Therefore, when I see the wonder of the transformational effect of snow, I am very excited because I know that my Father, the Lord, is about His usual business of transforming lives, families, cities and nations in the twinkling of an eye. It gives me the confidence of knowing that there is nothing that God cannot do, nor is there anything too hard for God, nor any situation too difficult. In a short space of time, He would transform a life - a destiny, a nations or even nations. This has been my experience repeatedly.

In 1989, in a short space of time, Communism fell and ended after 70 years. For over 70 years, communism had held many nations and lives in bondage, yet in a short space of time, all of that ceased and transformation came. The transformation of you the reader will come too, if you can trust God for that.

In a number of months in 2011/2012, we saw long reigning rulers and dictators fall one after another in the Middle East – during the so-called the Arab Spring.

In one day, Joseph the dreamer was transformed from prisoner and slave to prime minister. In one day, he changed his residence from prison to palace. In one day, transformation came and the slave became the head of a nation, the lowest became the highest. Only our God, the same God who transformed the landscape by snow, can make that happen.

In less than one year after a lifetime of waiting, a woman of Shunem became the mother of a son even though she was fulfilled having accepted the seeming inevitability of barrenness.

In 24 hours, the City of Samaria, which was under a siege so terrible that some began to eat their children, entered incredible freedom and wealth. Elisha the man of God, declared that in one day, a great breakthrough would come, the siege would be lifted and food would be sold for next to nothing. In the midst of such terrible siege, it was too much news for anyone to believe. Indeed one of the officials of the king openly challenged Elisha's declaration and prophecy. He wondered how such a transformation could happen in one day! He had not understood the secret of the snowy day. He said that even if God was to open the floodgates of heaven, he could not see how there would be such a transformation in 24 hours. (2 Kings 6:24-20; 2 King 7:1-3; 18-20).

It happened exactly as the prophet said, in one day, surplus became the order of the day.

When I see the snow, I learn the lesson about the

wonderful transforming power of a wonderful God. I learn that He can bring transformation to a life, a family, a church, or a nation or nations, in minutes, one day, one week, one month, one year, or in one season. I am confident that your transformation will not tarry because the Lord's programme does not need a long time. He can transform and will transform your destiny in a short while. It was the snow type of transformation that caused the psalmist to write Psalm 126 (KJV).

> *When the LORD turned again the captivity of Zion, we were like them that dream. Then was our mouth filled with laughter, and our tongue with singing: then said they among the heathen, The LORD hath done great things for them. The LORD hath done great things for us; whereof we are glad. Turn again our captivity, O LORD, as the streams in the south. They that sow in tears shall reap in joy. He that goeth forth and weepeth, bearing precious seed, shall doubtless come again with rejoicing, bringing his sheaves with him.*

Snowfall brings transformation. Heaven's floodgates are opened and the transforming power of God is poured out. In a short period, everything changes.

For those who have given up, your transformation is around the corner. In a short space of time, the glory of our great God will overshadow and overwhelm you. His snowfall will cause health to overwhelm every form of sickness, disease, lack and disorder.

CHAPTER 4

SNOWDY DAY CONFIRMS THAT THERE ARE INEXHAUSTIBLE STOREHOUSES IN HEAVEN

"Have you entered the storehouses of the snow or seen the storehouses of the hail..." (Job 38:22 NIV)

Having lived in Scotland for about seven years and witnessed many winters, the winter of 2009-2010 was a novel experience. By mid-January 2010, we had experienced about four weeks of almost continuous snowfall. It was anything but a typical winter.

Typically, the snow would fall for about one day or a few hours, set on the ground for a few more hours or days and then melt after that. However, this was different! The snowfall went on almost continuously for over four weeks. One began to ask when and whether the snow would not finish from its supply. The supply surely has to run out!

Not So! The snow kept on falling, day after day, week after week. Instead of the snow supply from the heavens running out, the resources and ability of governments to manage the winter days began to run out. Governments and councils ran out of grit, salt and scrapers. Shops ran out of salt, even energy was threatening to run out, yet the snow kept falling and there was no foreseen end to the snowfall.

The earth is transformed in the twinkling of an eye. How did that happen? Where does snow come from? How is it that there is so much of snow that within one hour the entire landscape could be changed and transformed?

Where was the snow before it began to fall? Rain, we can understand a wee bit; science explains that rain falls when the clouds are heavy enough with moisture. But snow? Where does it come from? Where is the supply from? The Lord gives us a glimpse of the secret of the snow: He has a storehouse full of snow! His supply is endless and countless, very unlike earthly or governmental storehouses or man's storehouses which are finite.

> *"Have you ever travelled to where snow is made, seen the vault where hail is stockpiled, the arsenals of hail and snow that I keep in readiness for times of trouble and battle and war? Can you find your way to where lightning is launched, or to the place from which the wind blows" Job 38:22 (MSG)*

From the above scripture, we get a deeper understanding. Snow is manufactured in the heavens where there are great storehouses full of snow. When it is time, the storehouse of snow is emptied upon a certain part of the earth to transform it.

When I see the snow, I get very excited because that confirms to me in a powerful and vivid way that heaven's storehouses of snow have been opened over a place, city or country. If there are inexhaustible storehouses of snow in the heavens, what other storehouses are there in heaven?

Then I discover that the the heavenly realm is full of wonderful storehouses:
• Storehouses of snow
• Storehouses and floodgates of blessing. (Malachi 3:10)
• Storehouses of healing
• Storehouses of babies
• Storehouses of righteousness (Psalms 36:6; 71:19; Isaiah 45:8; Amos 5:24; Malachi 4:2; Matthew 5:6)
• Storehouses of peace (Malachi 2:5; Numbers 25:12; Judges 3:11-30, 5:311, 6:24, 8:28; 1 Kings 5:4; 1 Chronicles 22:9; Psalms 29:11, 37:11, 85:10,119:165; Proverbs 16:7; John 14:27; 16:33; Ephesians 2:14; Philippians 4:7; 2 Thessalonians 3:16; Hebrews13:20)
• Storehouses of provision
• Storehouses of protection and preservation

Heaven is full of floodgates, not just storehouses. For

every good thing that pertains to life and godliness, Heaven has not just a storehouse but floodgates of them (Ephesians 1:3). Heaven is full of floodgates of blessings, children, health, deliverance, breakthrough, and we also know that when the Lord opens his floodgates of snow, the earth would be overwhelmed and cannot get enough of snow. In similar fashion, I got more excited to know that the Lord can and does also open the floodgates of blessings and overwhelm some of his children - He made this promise in Malachi 3:10-12 MSG:

> *Lord, open your floodgates of blessing and shower your children blessings that are so overwhelming they cannot comprehend or handle them!*

When you see the snow falling, pouring forth down from heaven's storehouse, you are seeing a vivid confirmation that there are great storehouses in heaven filled with every blessing and everything that pertains to life and godliness. Next, I want to thank Him for opening the floodgates. And my hope and expectation are increasing!

CHAPTER 5

THERE IS A MEASURE AND A FLOODING

It is exciting to know that not only does heaven have storehouses of blessings, the Lord in His infiniteness can and does order the floodgates to be opened over a person, people, church, city or nation. In the past, we have enjoyed snow in some measure, but in the year 2010, we saw snow in overwhelming and overflowing volumes. Certainly, it was just not a case of the storehouse of snow being opened over us for a measure of snowfall, but it was as it was as if the Lord decreed that the floodgates of snow be opened.

Now we understand that heaven can rain down blessings and supplies from the great storehouses above. We also understand that sometimes and for some people, the blessing does not just rain, it becomes an overwhelming flood as we see in Malachi 3:10:

> *Bring the whole tithe into the storehouse, that there*
> *may be food in my house. Test me in this," says the*
> LORD *Almighty, "and see if I will not throw open the*

floodgates of heaven and pour out so much blessing that you will not have room enough for it.

And Ephesians 3:20:
Now to him who is able to do immeasurably more than all we ask or imagine, according to his power that is at work within us.
What really gets me excited is that sometimes, and for some people, heaven pours out supplies from the great storehouse. Then there are other times and seasons when heaven opens the floodgates of blessings and the storehouses just pour and rain blessings on some individuals! That is one of the promises made to tithe-payers.. If you are a tithe-payer, you are guaranteed to experience and enjoy God's blessings without measure.
In the memorable winter, the Lord opened not just the door to the storehouse of snows but ordered the floodgates to overwhelm the land with an over-abundance of snow. In the similar fashion, I pray the heavens to flood you the reader with the blessings of heaven. Believers enjoy the blessings of God in different measures but it is the right of tithe-payers not just to enjoy measures of blessings, but to enjoy an over-flow of blessings.

Prayer

- *Lord, thank you for your great and many blessings in our lives.*
- *We have seen what you do to the land with the snow during deep winter seasons when you pour out overabundance of snow from the inexhaustible supplies of heaven. Please overwhelm us in this season with the floodgates of Heaven*
- *Please cause an avalanche of blessings to fall on every tithe-payer. This is a season for open floodgates; let every tithe-payer enjoy your overwhelming flood of blessings.*

CHAPTER 6

THE SNOW WHITE WASH

It is amazing to see the power and ability of snow to transform land, landscapes, towns and villages. There is a neighbourhood – lets call that Jamesville - I know that ordinarily is derelict, dilapidated and run-down... This neighbourhood is full of litter, abandoned and scrap cars, altogether creating a depressing picture.

Yet when the snowfalls, the neighbourhood is transformed. When snow falls, ugly-looking rooftops are covered in sheets of white. Cars are buried under heaps of snow. You can no longer tell what make or model any car is, nor can you tell whether the car was nice or terrible, functional or abandoned. As a matter of fact, if this was your first visit to that neighbourhood covered in snow, you would not know it is ordinarily in such bad state. This is the wonderful transforming power of snow. If the same community or area was to remain permanently covered by snow, these neighbourhoods would be permanently changed.

Many of our lives are much like the state of the neighbourhood of Jamesville; scrappy and derelict in many areas including fractured relationships with family, people and God. You can tell that life does not seem to be going anywhere.

You may know someone with an unsavoury history and you keep your distance only to hear that the chap has found God. The man had an encounter with God and gradually and yet surely, his life is changed and turned around completely. The next time you meet him, you cannot understand it! He has changed! In appearance, behaviour, and relationship and in every way - the chap has become a model citizen! What happened?

The cleansing power of God and the blood of Jesus has been at work! When a life is handed to the Lord, he is able to bring about such overwhelming transformation that the final picture is even more dramatic than the story of Jamesville before and after the avalanche of snow.

No wonder, the man and king David who was pretty much like Jamesville - , a cheat, an adulterer, who ordered the murder of his mistress's innocent and unsuspecting husband. When he came to his senses, he cried to God in repentance and asked for the snowfall-type of change and transformation.

Soak me in your laundry and I'll come out clean, scrub

me and I'll have a snow-white life. (Psalms 51:7 MSG)
So many lives appear successful and yet inwardly
tormented and in pain and constant insecurity! Many like
David, should cry to the Lord in desperation asking him
to transform their lives. (Psalms 51:1-19 MSG)

*   Have you been to Jesus for the cleansing power?
*   Are you washed in the blood of the lamb?
*   Are your garments spotless are they white as snow?
*   Are you washed in the blood of the lamb?

When I see the snow, I know and remember that my life,
our lives, can be sorted out and transformed by God and
become all-sparkling like the snow-covered landscapes
no matter the dirt, mess and decay that was previously
the case.

> *"Come. Sit down. Let's argue this out." This is God's
> Message: "If your sins are blood-red, they'll be snow-
> white. If they're red like crimson, they'll be like wool"
> (Isaiah 1:18-19MSG)*

CHAPTER 7

A GLIMPSE OF THE GLORY OF HEAVEN

At higher heights and peaks, snow on the landscape looks particularly glorious. It is very lovely and it produces much fun and excitement from children building snowmen to sledging down hills and skating on frozen lakes. The snowy day has a glory and spectacle about it. In many parts of the scripture, the garment of the most High Lord of all creation, the King of kings is indescribable, but it can best be described as similar to snow.

So I get an understanding much like Martin Luther aptly described marriage as God's best way of expressing Himself and the relationship with His church. I get to understand that the glory and glitter of the snow is perhaps the best or nearest that the human eye can comprehend of the glory of God.

As I was watching all this,
"Thrones were set in place and The Old One sat down. His robes were white as snow; his hair was

> *white like wool. His throne was flaming with fire, its wheels blazing. A river of fire poured out of the throne. Thousands upon thousands served him, tens of thousands attended him. The courtroom was called to order, and the books were opened. (Dan 7:9 MSG)*

The angel who rolled the stone away on resurrection morning was clothed in a garment with a colour best expressed as snow-white.

> *… Suddenly the earth reeled and rocked under their feet as God's angel came down from heaven, came right up to where they were standing. He rolled back the stone and then sat on it. Shafts of lightning blazed from him. His garments shimmered snow-white. The guards at the tomb were scared to death. They were so frightened, they couldn't move. (Matt 28:3)*

At the mountain of transfiguration, the garment of our Lord Jesus also became snow-white, shinning, glittering white, whiter than any bleach could whiten cloths. Three of the disciples saw it. Jesus took Peter, James, and John and led them up a high mountain. His appearance changed from the inside out, right before their eyes. His clothes shimmered, glistening white, whiter than any bleach could make them. (Mark 9:3)

Revelations 1:14 described the hair of the son of man as being white, like wool and as snow.

His head and hair were white like wool, as white as snow, and his eyes were like blazing fire." *(Revelations 1:14 NIV)*

What a glorious spectacle we see of winter - I am very excited that the spectacle, colour, whiteness is the nearest representation of the garment of the Ancient of Days, His Son, the angels and perhaps that will also be the colour of our heavenly garment. What exciting thoughts! Therefore, when I see the glory of a snow-clad mountain top, or the landscape, the whiteness no bleach can produce, I believe that I am getting a glimpse of garment of the Holy One.

Moses spent forty days and forty nights, with the Lord on the mountain. By the time he came back, Moses' face was so radiant and glorious that people were afraid to go near him. The radiance beyond that of luscious snow on a high mountaintop was upon Moses and people were afraid to see his face.

When Moses came down from Mount Sinai carrying the two Tablets of The Testimony, he didn't know that the skin of his face glowed because he had been speaking with GOD. Aaron and all the Israelites who saw Moses, saw his radiant face, and held back, afraid to get close to him. (Exodus 34: 29-30)

Prayer
- *Lord, help me! I want to see more of you, more of your glory!*
- *I want to see more of you in my life.*

CHAPTER 8

HANDLE WITH CARE

Afriend, during the winter of 2010, was on his way to work. As the roads were quite icy and dangerous. Instead of riding his scooter as he normally would, he decided to use public transport, On his way to the bus stop, he slid on the ice and broke his arm. Trying to be safe on a snowy day, he still ended up with an accident.

One question perplexed me. If snow is so glorious, a blessing from heaven, a reflection or resemblance of God's glory why is it that many times, when snow comes down, much care is required for walking on the streets, taking buses, driving and for practically every otherwise ordinary outdoor activity.? If not carefully managed, the aftermath of snow can produce quite disastrous consequences. So the question perplexed me, If snow is glorious, why the potential damage, the disruptions and in some cases, death?

Then I got an understanding from; Moses was a dear friend of Lord. A time came that he sought to get even closer to the Lord to know his ways, to have his continuous presence and to see His glory. The Lord told him that no man can see his face and still live so he would allow Moses to catch a glimpse not of his face but of his back.

The presence of God and His glory is radiant, exciting and beautiful but also dangerous. So also is the paradox of the snowy day. Miriam the sister of Moses offended against the Lord and her brother Moses, she found out to her sorrow that the glory and the presence of the Lord could also be mightily dangerous. When she offended When the Lord responded in His glorious displeasure, he left a mark on Miriam - leprosy as white as snow! The radiance of snow was there as usual but it produced a terrible result for Miriam because her actions displeased Him.

I learn therefore that the snowy day as with the glory of the Lord, needs to be beheld with care and deep respect. If a man or woman treats the Lord or his matters carnally, casually or with outright disrespect, there will be terrible consequences. In a similar fashion, a person who decides to treat the Lord and His matters with respect and clear consideration can quickly find comfort and help in difficult circumstances.

The society will do well to treat the Ancient of Days, God's house and matters with great respect. Many assume the Lord to be a harmless Father Christmas-like figure. Many countries, states, governments, churches and individuals appear to think of the Holy One as an anachronism or an unwanted controller that has been outgrown. That is playing with danger in similar fashion to carelessness on a snowy day. Part of the decline of western values results from the manner of treating the Holy One and his affairs with levity. As someone once asked, *"We spend plenty of time on human rights, state rights, animal rights, the rights of the minority, but what about God's Rights?"* We have created a false world in which we think man is in control and we can do whatever we like and then when disaster comes, we then ask why God allow this or that disaster?

As with snowy day, you are best advised to handle the Lord, the Holy One, whose garment is purer and whiter than snow, with the utmost respect. Just as it is dangerous to be exposed unprotected to the wrath of cold, ice and snow, it is a more dangerous to fall into the wrath of the living God. (Hebrews 12:13-28 MSG)

Many people, including evangelical and born-again Christians, give the Lord very little respect. As a matter of fact, many of us give Him less respect than we give our friends, spouses, employers and supervisors at work. Perhaps, it is because He is not immediately visible to the naked eye. For one reason or the other, we behave disrespectfully to the Mighty One. This level of disrespect is so perplexing that it generates a thoughtful discussion; the Lord had to ask His people about their gross disrespect in Malachi 1:1-13.

A son gives honour to his father, and a servant has fear of his master: if then I am a father, where is my honour? and if I am a master, where is the fear of me? says the Lord of armies to you, O priests, who give no value to my name. And you say, How have we not given value to your name? You put unclean bread on my altar. And you say, How have we made it unclean? By your saying, The table of the Lord is of no value. And when you give what is blind for an offering, it is no evil! and when you give what is damaged and ill, it is no evil! Give it now to your ruler; will he be pleased with you, or will you have his approval? says the Lord of armies.

The snow is glorious, wonderful and all fluffy but it must be respected otherwise it is dangerous and could be harmful to anyone that does not approach it with decorum. It is even more so the case with the God of heaven even though He is all loving, all forgiving, and awesome. Do you see how thankful we must be? We should not only be thankful, but also brimming with worship and be deeply reverent before God for God is not an indifferent bystander. He is actively cleaning the life and the house, removing all that needs to be burnt up - He won't quit until it's all cleansed. God himself is Fire! (Hebrews 12:29 MSG)

Again, we see the dangers of treating the Almighty and the things of God and his church with levity in 1 Corinthians 11:23-33b.

So, my friends, when you come together to the Lord's Table, be reverent and courteous with one another. If you're so hungry that you can't wait to be served, go home and get a sandwich. But by no means risk turning this Meal into an eating and drinking binge or a family squabble. It is a spiritual meal — a love feast. (1 Corinthians 11:33a-33b MSG)

Lets us walk circumspectly before the Lord. Let us give him the honour and respect due him. When God's people honour him, it leads to expansive growth of the church but dishonouring Him exposes society to decay and every manner of error. There is one vivid illustration of folks who dishonour Him.

God did extraordinary miracles through Paul, so that even handkerchiefs and aprons that had touched him were taken to the sick, and their illnesses were cured and the evil spirits left them. Some Jews who went around driving out evil spirits tried to invoke the name of the Lord Jesus over those who were demon-possessed. They would say, "In the name of Jesus, whom Paul preaches, I command you to come out." Seven sons of Sceva, a Jewish chief priest, were doing this. (One day) the evil spirit answered them, "Jesus I know, and I know about Paul, but who are you?" Then the man who had the evil spirit jumped on them and overpowered them all. He gave them such a beating that they ran out of the house naked and bleeding. When this became known to the Jews and Greeks living in Ephesus, they were all seized with fear, and the name of the Lord Jesus was held in high honour. (Acts 19:11-17 NIV)

CHAPTER 9

THE DAY FOR EXPLOITS – THE SNOWY DAY REVEALS PEOPLE OF EXPLOITS

One of my most favourite characters in the scriptures is the man named Benaiah. He was one of David's men and companions. The guy Benaiah was, to put it mildly and simply, a "crazy guy". Let's read a little bit about Benaiah and his "radicalism".

Benaiah son of Jehoiada was a valiant fighter from Kabzeel, who performed great exploits. He struck down two of Moab's best men. He also went down into a pit on a snowy day and killed a lion. And he struck down an Egyptian who was seven and a half feet tall. Although the Egyptian had a spear like a weaver's rod in his hand, Benaiah went against him with a club. He snatched the spear from the Egyptian's hand and killed him with his own spear. Such were the exploits of Benaiah son of Jehoiada; he too was as famous as the three mighty men. He was held in greater honour than any of the Thirty, but he was not included among the Three. And David put him in charge of his bodyguard. (1 Chronicles 11:22-25 NIV)

Ten Things About Benaiah
BENAIAH WAS PART OF A "CRAZY" GANG – THAT WAS COMPLETELY SOLD OUT TO THE LORD

You will agree with me that Benaiah was crazy in an excellent way. Thinking again, that makes excellent sense because David who was their leader was himself crazy, having confronted a giant as well. How else would you describe a 17-year-old boy taking up the challenge to an older and very experienced soldier giant with armour, shield, swords and even a shield bearer? It was crazy enough for the teenager to take up the challenge that had been on for forty days. It was crazy for a teenager to take up a challenge that all the professional army would not dare. It was even crazier to see the teenager go against the experienced fighting machine called Goliath, with just a sling and five stones in his pocket. David was a crazy sort of guy. No wonder most of his close lieutenants and associates turned out to be a crazy set of people as well.

The friends or company that a person keeps is very important. If the people you hang around are not going anywhere or are not high achievers, it is very likely that you will not be a high achiever. If you mingle with high achievers, it is only a matter of time before you become a high achiever. If a person keeps company with scrupulous people, it is likely that that individual will be scrupulous. Truly, the scripture declares that 'evil communication corrupts good manners' (1Corinthians 15.33). Benaiah and his companions were the lowest of the low when they started off.

> *David therefore departed thence, and escaped to the cave Adullam: and when his brethren and all his father's house heard it, they went down thither to him. And every one that was in distress, and every one that was in debt, and every one that was discontented, gathered themselves unto him; and he became a captain over them: and there were with him about four hundred men. (1 Samuel 22.1-2 KJV)*

Benaiah and his companions were, in the beginning, the lowest of the low in the society. Then, they saw a young man who loved God and was doing exploits for God. They saw a man who seemingly came from nowhere to rise to prominence and they were smart enough to join up with him. They wanted to walk and live with David and one by one, the lowest started going away to be with David. Benaiah yearned to be somebody and so he joined David as well. Over time, he became a leader and David's companion; he also became a man of great exploits.

David's men were an interesting lot. These were men who just loved to have a fight for good causes, men for whom risk was nothing. They were ever ready to take up a challenge. This is evident in how Jebus was taken. All David did, was to raise a challenge, whoever would go first and conquer would become Chief of Staff of the Army. David's men were always challenged to do exploits. See 1 Chronicles 11:5, 6

It is great wisdom for a man or woman to seek and keep the company of people going places. Conversely, it is undiscerning and rather stupid for a man to stay with people who have no high ambition or people who do not aspire for greatness. Benaiah became a man of exploits because he sought and joined the company of men who did exploits. He did not become a man of exploits simply by chance. Greatness is contagious. Smallness is also contagious.

Consider some of the craziness and exploits of some of David's men by reading 1 Chronicles 11:4-25 (NIV) which will lead to the next point.

BENAIAH BECAME SKILFUL
David, though only a shepherd and a teenager at the time he took up the challenge of confronting Goliath, had mastery of slingshots and catapults. Though he had no experience with the sword or armour, he was extremely skilful at throwing the slingshot. He only needed one shot at Goliath, and he had the giant down and out! There was no need for a second shot.

We need to be extremely skilful at what we do already. We need also to acquire new skills. Do you clean floors? Become an expert at cleaning floors. Do you cook? Become an expert in cooking. David's men did not start off as such but they became people of great skill. Many unfortunately, in God's house, are not faithful in our work places or in relationships. We hear about folks who are not faithful at work. If you are not faithful over a few things, then who will give you greater things?

CASE STUDY - I know a friend from way back. He was working as a top engineer with an international oil company. In his local church, he started the church bookshop. He did it so well that he eventually also started a Christian bookshop in his local city. That bookshop eventually became very successful. He has since left the oil industry and to gone on become a great bookseller, becoming very rich and successful at that. He became successful at what he knew to do.

Friends, brothers and sisters, it is time to be highly skilful in what we do. The kingdom of God is in need of many skills.

Benaiah was described as a valiant warrior. 'Valiant' comes from the Hebrew word *'chayil'* which means strength, ability, efficiency and is descriptive of an army. We need to be military-like in our abilities. The military is known first for the boot camp where new joiners are first trained and indoctrinated. Training, dedication and complete focus are some of the attributes of an army. We need to become military-like in our focus, skill and discipline. Choose and focus on one or two skills, become thoroughly expert at it. Let everyone around you know about your focus, discipline and your passion.

These are the men who joined David in Ziklag; it was during the time he was banished by Saul the son of Kish; they were among the Mighty Men, good fighters. They were armed with bows and could sling stones and shoot arrows either right or left-handed. They hailed from Saul's tribe, Benjamin. (1Chronicles 12:1-2 MSG)

BENAIAH WAS COMPLETELY COMMITTED AND TRUSTWORTHY

There were some Gadites there who had defected to David at his wilderness fortress; they were seasoned and eager fighters who knew how to handle shield and spear. They were wild in appearance, like lions, but as agile as gazelles racing across the hills. Ezer was the first, then Obadiah, Eliab, Mishmannah, Jeremiah, Attai, Eliel, Johanan, Elzabad, Jeremiah, and Macbannai – eleven of them. These Gadites were the cream of the crop – any one of them was worth a hundred lesser men, and the best of them were worth a thousand. They were the ones who crossed the Jordan when it was at flood stage in the first month, and put everyone in the lowlands to flight, both east and west. (1 Chronicles 12:8-15 MSG)

Once Benaiah and the others signed up with David, there was no looking back - there was no room to go back. They were committed to David and the Lord's business. I appeal to God's people, let us become super committed. Some people lose their commitment and focus for many reasons, some of which are because of hardship, sentiments or because of challenges.

One of the complications of life for us today is the issue of commitment. Many of us are not committed to what God has given to us. It was once reported from a study of marriages in India - I got to discover a shocking truth, that most of the marriages in India are arranged marriages; the spouses are chosen by their parents and the people to be married do not have a say in the matter. Now the intriguing part is that one would expect that such marriages would not last. Alas, statistics show that the rate of divorce in India is very low compared to other parts of the world! This is simply because they have a commitment of 100 percent, but on the contrary, people that choose for themselves, even Christians, despite the fact that they are aware that God doesn't support divorce, still go ahead to get divorced. One fundamental reason is the lack of total commitment to the cause. The level of commitment a man shows, determines the extent to which he will go. Lack of commitment is one of the complications that God cannot abide. Where is your commitment? People who would do exploits MUST be committed, super committed.

Not all who wanted to join David were accepted. Some men tried to join David but their commitment was in question, they could not be trusted:

> *Some from the tribe of Manasseh also defected to David when he started out with the Philistines to go to war against Saul. In the end, they didn't actually fight because the Philistine leaders, after talking it over, sent them home, saying, "We can't trust them with our*

> *lives – they'll betray us to their master Saul."   (1*
> *Chronicles 12:19 MSG)*

Yet and most interestingly, some of King Saul's kinsmen defected to David and convinced David of their steadfastness and commitment and David accepted them.

BENAIAH WAS PART OF AN EVER INCREASING GANG

Benaiah and his colleagues in David's army were a group to whom the Lord added daily. They increased daily until they became a mighty army. Each also increased individually – increasing in strength, ability and their commitment to God. They were leaders and men who were deepening their walk with the Lord and increasing in faith and holiness! We have a responsibility to seek to increase in every aspect of our lives. There should be no staleness, stagnation or vacuum in your life. Keep studying. Keep increasing. God needs us to keep increasing. Don't become stagnant!

> *The men from Manasseh who defected to David at Ziklag were Adnah, Jozabad, Jediael, Michael, Jozabad, Elihu, and Zillethai, all leaders among the families of Manasseh. They helped David in his raids against the desert bandits; they were all stalwart fighters and good leaders among his raiders. Hardly a day went by without men showing up to help – it wasn't long before his band seemed as large as God's own army! (1Chronicle12: 20-22 MSG)*

BENAIAH'S FOCUS WAS THE LORD GOD - NO SECTIONAL TRIBAL OR PAROCHIAL SENTIMENTS

One main reason why Benaiah and his companions joined David in the wilderness, in the cave of Adullam, was that they knew that the call of God was upon David and he was fighting God's battles. They did not join David because of mere sentiment, nationalism, emotions or self-interest (although there was some of that). They joined David because they saw a man whose heart was right towards God and men. Abigail confirmed this when she declared to David:

> *I pray thee, forgive the trespass of thine handmaid: for the LORD will certainly make my Lord a sure house; because my Lord fighteth the battles of the LORD, and evil hath not been found in thee all thy days. Yet a man is risen to pursue thee, and to seek thy soul: but the soul of my Lord shall be bound in the bundle of life with the LORD thy God; and the souls of thine enemies, them shall he sling out, as out of the middle of a sling. And it shall come to pass, when the LORD shall have done to my Lord according to all the good that he hath spoken concerning thee, and shall have appointed thee ruler over Israel; (1 Samuel 25:28-30 KJV)*

Those who will be part of the Lord's "radical" team have no room for sectional, tribal, nationalistic or parochial sentiments. Those are baser instincts. God's army has no room or place for such base instincts.

HE KNEW THAT DAVID WAS GOING SOMEWHERE

Benaiah knew he was going somewhere, if he was with the Lord and with David. The rest of David's band knew they were going somewhere. The folks knew that David was a man that the Lord was taking somewhere. They knew that they, as part of David's band, were themselves going somewhere and that helped them to be focused.

Do you know that God is taking you somewhere? Some do not know and appreciate that and therefore they easily get distracted and sidetracked. The people of this world are so wise in this regard that they will join themselves to and serve people who can take them anywhere, no matter how terrible the destination or the motivation. As a result there are many people in gangs, cults, criminal, terrorist and secret organisations because they have been promised help, preferment, favour, fellowship, all in an evil manner and for short-term prosperity. However, we in the Lord have the true and real stuff. The Lord is really taking us somewhere! The non-entities who went to join David at Ziklag became a mighty army (1 Samuel 22:1-2).

BENAIAH WENT DOWN

From the place of God's presence, we ought to go out into the world to solve problems. It is not enough to only stay in God's presence, or to enjoy communion with the Lord or to pray only. From the high place of God's presence, we are designed and expected "to go down!" - not to go down to sin or trouble but rather to get down and confront the challenges facing the world.

We see from the example of Moses that he went up to the Mount of God, to commune and receive from the Lord the Ten Commandments. Then he "came down" to pass God's purpose and message on to His nation and generation. David would commune with the Lord and then he would go out to war and do according to the instructions received in the place of prayer and communion with the Lord. The Lord's presence is the headquarters. From HQ, we get our instructions then we must then go down, hit the streets, the marketplace, go to the nations to attend to the challenges, impact society for good and win for Him.

There is no victory without 'going down' to battle the challenges of our generation.

Benaiah heard that there was a lion threatening the peace of his community and so he got up and went down to confront the lion. On another occasion, he heard that an Egyptian giant was threatening the peace of his community. Again, he went down to confront the Egyptian. He fought, defeated and killed the giant.

The world is waiting for the sons and daughters of God to come down and confront the challenges of their society.

> *"For the strong desire of every living thing is waiting for the revelation of the sons of God." (Ro 8.19 BEB)*

Concerning our Lord Jesus, it is recorded that: "When he had come down from the mountain, great multitudes followed him ..." (Matthew 8:1). The mountain or high place can be likened to the very presence of God and 'down' can be likened to the world and its challenges.

It is a good prayer to say: *Lord, help me henceforth, to continue in your presence, yet go out to confront the challenges of my generation.*

BENAIAH WENT TO SLAY A LION IN THE PIT ON A SNOWY DAY

Benaiah must have heard of a lion was about and a threat to the community – he heard that the threatening lion had fallen into a pit. Everyone probably was afraid in the town and was speaking about it in hushed tones until Benaiah heard that a fearful thing had happened in the town square - a lion was threatening the people. Without thinking twice Benaiah got out of his house, even though it was a snowy day and normally a day to be cosy and warm at home – not so for him – if there was a threat, it was a day for battle. He went out to confront and defeat the lion. He went to take away the threat facing his community. He confronted and overcame the challenge facing his generation.

The people of God are designed with the mind of God, to transform society and answer every threat facing our generation. Be it drugs, alcoholism or sexual immorality, we are the ones the world is waiting for to solve problems. Like Benaiah, we should leave our comfort zone to confront and defeat the "lions" that are threats to our generations.

The "lion" can be likened to any threat facing the society. Our society and generation is waiting for the manifestation of the Benaiahs of our time who would confront and solve the challenges of today. *For the earnest expectation of the creation eagerly waits for the manifestation of the sons of God.* (Romans 8.19)

What are the lions of my generation, you may ask? Which would I take responsibility for? Sports, business, or media? We are to take responsibility for all I must add. We should influence whatever field we can. For example, the chap who ministers to top Christian footballers and other sports people. He teaches them how to make an impact for the Lord.

BENAIAH WENT ON A SNOWY DAY

Like Benaiah, we are called to battle for the Lord. The battle is a fierce one and there is no comfort zone as we are called to fight whether it is convenient or not. We are called to be constant in or out of season. Battle in and out of season. Preach the word in season and out of season; reprove, rebuke, exhort with all longsuffering and doctrine (2 Timothy 4:2)

BENAIAH LIKE THE REST OF DAVID'S BAND, WAS AN UNREASONABLE MAN

This world is unreasonable. Or how else could one describe a place where right is replaced with wrong? How else could you describe a place where contrary to even animal instinct, society says a man can marry a man? How else could one describe a place where alcohol and drugs are celebrated? How else could you describe a place where those who honour and revere the Lord are marginalised?

The unreasonableness of the world so perplexed the writer of Ecclesiastes in Chapter 10 verses 5-7 that he wrote:

> *There is an evil which I have seen under the sun, as an error which proceeds from the ruler: Folly is set in great dignity, and the rich sit in low place. I have seen servants upon horses, and princes walking as servants upon the earth.*

The world is an unreasonable place and those who get by in the world are unreasonable people, yet many Christians insist on being reasonable in an unreasonable world!
Do you know how people try to be reasonable? Being calm, collected and not rocking the boat! How so wrong! To meet the challenges of our generation for the Lord, we must become "unreasonable people" like Benaiah, doing strange and perplexing things.

No doubt, you would now agree that David, Benaiah and the rest of David's men were a type of people uncommon to the world:
- Men of great exploits
- Men who knew no fear
- Men who did not regard death

- Men who dared risk
- Men who defied reason

It is time for the co-heirs of the son of David to become thoroughly crazy for the King; it is time again for crazy folks to arise. It is time to be uncommon!

Do we not need proactive folks?
Benaiah was certainly one radical chap, like David his leader, and very much like his fellows and companions. However, Benaiah's craziness is aptly captured by one of his unique doings.

Imagine a snowy day: cold, freezing, snow everywhere, roads and paths slippery with ice. This is not a day for going out. if it can be helped, one ideally should stay indoors instead, Benaiah goes out of his house to fight a lion in a public pit on a cold, slippery, snowy day! The lion was already in a pit so he could have left the lion there if it was harming no one, however, that was not the type of person that Benaiah was. On that snowy day, when all reasonable men and women were in bed or at home snuggling in front of the fire, Benaiah went out to take up the challenge of the lion that was in the wrong place and perhaps a threat to the society. He went out, went into the pit where the lion was and fought it for victory.

Benaiah was not a reasonable man. The snowy day was the day for exploits. The snowy day may symbolise the inconvenient day, the unique challenges and threats that confront the society, the Lord's church and the land. The snowy day symbolises that many of the challenges are so hard and difficult looking that reasonable men and women act reasonably and stay at home.

Being full of faith is unreasonable when a man disbelieves tangible fact and insist on holding on to faith – disbelieving the physical and believing the spiritual - that is humanly speaking unreasonable.

But Benaiah, like David his leader, and his companions had learnt to be unreasonable and crazy people for God. David was not reasonable by going to fight the giant Goliath when no trained, experienced and reasonable soldier in the army would go forward. Reason said that Goliath was too much of a giant to be confronted and defeated, but David was not a reasonable teenager, he was a teenager inbred with the Spirit of God.

The Spirit of God is beyond reason. The Spirit of God is not the spirit of reason but the Spirit of Faith. The people of God from the beginning have been called unusual, unreasonable and "crazy" for doing exploits for the Lord, their church, land and family.

> *Here am I, and the children the LORD has given me. We are signs and symbols in Israel from the LORD Almighty, who dwells on Mount Zion (Isaiah 8:18 NIV).*

The people of God are for signs and wonders in Israel. We are called to do exploits for the kingdom and not to conform to the norm. Our Lord and saviour Jesus was more than a type of David. David foreshadowed some of what he would do in his earthly ministry.

He was an unreasonable man on an uncommon mission. In selecting His lieutenants, He chose unreasonable men, the unlikeliest of men.

1. He was an unreasonable man on an uncommon mission.
2. In selecting His lieutenants, He chose unreasonable men, the unlikeliest of men.
3. He was born in the most unreasonable place for a king - in a manager, with animals.
4. His earthly ministry was unreasonably short in human thought - only three and half years.
5. Everything he did was unreasonable, He appointed the unlikeliest group of men and women and handed the assignment of transforming the world to them.
6. Jesus' disciples were an unlikely lot - they were ordinary men, made unreasonable and extraordinary by the influence and power of God - so they turned the world rightside up!

Read: Acts 17:6; Luke 23:5; Acts 4:13-21 and Acts 4:13-14. "Unreasonable" Paul and Silas were held in prison. Reason would have meant they sleep, cry, moan or shout - but being unreasonable, they started a praise party at midnight

(Acts 16:25). The Bereans were unreasonable! In Acts 17:11-12 NIV, we read that they actually went to examine, re-examine and cross-examine what they heard the disciples say.

> *Now the Bereans were of more noble character than the Thessalonians, for they received the message with great eagerness and examined the Scriptures every day to see if what Paul said was true. Many of the Jews believed, as did also a number of prominent Greek women and many Greek men. Acts 17:11-12 NIV*

Paul and his companions stirred uproars as they performed great miracles and converts in every city that they went to. No city was immune; no town was too big or too small for Paul to turn upside down! In the city of Thessalonica, Paul caused uproar in the city (Acts17:5). When imprisoned, Paul and his companions caused heaven to send an earthquake to set them free (Acts 16:26). It was unreasonable Paul and the unreasonable people in Ephesus that had Bible studies daily for two years (Act 19: 9-12). Historians reckon that the Bible Studies were held in the hall of Tyrannus for about four hours daily mid morning to early afternoon. Paul chose the hours between 11 am and 3 pm, which were usually the break or siesta hour in the hot climate of Ephesus. That was unreasonable. No wonder the Bible recorded that in the same Ephesus, out of the ordinary, extra-ordinary miracles were recorded there (Acts 19:11).

- Paul also caused uproar in Ephesus (Acts19:23-34).
- In Acts 24:5, Paul like Jesus, was accused of trying to

turn the world upside down.
- It was unreasonable Esther, who risked her life to see the emperor in order to intervene to save the Jews!
- It was unreasonable for Mary Magdalene, who poured oil of unreasonable value, to anoint our Lord.

We, the people of God, are called to be people of exploits. We are called to be unreasonable people, to turn our cities "right-side up." What a collection of unreasonable and non-conforming people we are! Let us be added to the gallery of the names of unreasonable people of old for the Lord.

Therefore we learn the great truth that the snowy day teaches us, that the snowy day is a most reasonable day to be cosy and comfortable at home and comfortable, there are unreasonable men and women out on such unreasonable days and seasons doing exploits for the great King.

It is time for the *'SNOWY DAY CREW'* to rise and take the world for the Lord unreasonably.
- Unreasonable people are self-motivated
- They take up challenges unannounced
- Unreasonable folk go out
- Unreasonable folk do not wait for the "right season"

The snowy day, the day of change, shows up as the day of opportunity for men and women of exploits, unreasonable men and women.

"The reasonable man adapts himself to the world. The

unreasonable one persists in trying to adapt the world to himself. Therefore all progress depends on the unreasonable man."

The world system itself is unreasonable; therefore the person who insists on being reasonable in an unreasonable world is not really reasonable.

It is an unreasonable world system that says for example that a man can be joined to a man or a woman to a woman. That is ordinarily out of sync with logic, reason and nature. It is an unreasonable world system that says that sex, alcohol and drugs must be the preoccupation of many. The children of God are called not to be reasonable but to be smart, in fact smart and unreasonable in a world system that is itself unreasonable. It is folly therefore to insist on being reasonable in a world system that is itself unreasonable.

The people of God, like Benaiah, David, Paul and others in every generation are called:
- to break bonds
- to overthrow limits
- to do the impossible
- to outwit the witty
- to outdo the boundless
- to "outwise" the wisdom of the world
- and much more

The children of God are called not to be reasonable but to be unreasonable; not to be people of reason but to be people of faith (Luke 8:25). In Luke 10:13-15, Jesus commented on the damaging unreasonableness of the world system. He also lamented at the insistence of the children of God on being reasonable in an unreasonable world system

> *"Now here's a surprise: The master praised the crooked manager! And why? Because he knew how to look after himself. Streetwise people are smarter in this regard than law-abiding citizens. They are on constant alert, looking for angles, surviving by their wits. I want you to be smart in the same way — but for what is right — using every adversity to stimulate you to creative survival, to concentrate your attention on the bare essentials, so you'll live, really live, and not complacently just get by on good behavior."* Luke 16:8-9 MSG)

JOIN THE SNOWY DAY CREW AND YOU WILL LIVE, REALLY LIVE AND NOT JUST GET BY ON GOOD BEHAVIOUR

EPILOGUE

THE BLESSINGS OF A SNOWY DAY

What is the winter season like? Is there someone who enjoys winter, the snow, even with all the slippery sidewalks, or the cold? Many people complain that winter is too cold, too fluffy, too much snow but we should have a different understanding, that winter snow is a blessing from God.

The Bible says in Psalm 147:16, that He gives snow like wool. There is a special blessing which the Lord has reserved for us. I imagined that really blessed hymn writer, who wrote that beautiful hymn *"How Great Thou Art"* when he saw the mountains and the hills, and the valleys and saw the snow. How the man must have just waxed the lyrics out and began to pen the words of the much loved hymn:
O Lord my God, when I in awesome wonder
consider all the work thy hands have made
I see the stars. I hear the rolling thunder.

Thy power throughout the universe displayed.
Then sings my soul, my saviour God to thee.
How great Thou art! How Great Thou art!

So do not see the snow as trouble, rather see it as a great blessing. The Bible says the Lord gives us snow. The snow comes from heaven's storehouses! He gives us snow for our great blessings! So you can go into the rest of the year with confidence that even the elements are working for your good.

Global warming is real: the earth is getting warmed up. Nothing unusual about that since right from the days of Adam to date, man has always exhibited the tendency to misuse what God gave to mankind! So no surprise about global warming! When God created the world and gave it to Adam, he misused it and since that time, it's always been the pattern of mankind to abuse and misuse global resources.

We need to go to od to learn how to rightly use the divine resources of heaven and the earth.

Global warming or no global warming, wintertime will continue, and God is saying this to you and I: *"My word would never fail, my promises always stand."* And that's why you can look at the snow and *know that the word of God will never fail. You can go back to the word of God now and say, "The word of God says that as long as the earth remains, there would be summer and winter." I have seen winter as I have*

*never seen it before, therefore, I know more than ever that the
word of God never fails, that God never fails!*

What word are you trusting God for? What is the word of
God for your own life? You can be sure that as long as
there is snow on the ground that is your own
confirmation that His Word would come to pass in your
own life. So if you go out, enjoy the snow and access the
spiritual dimensions of the snowy day.

 You are a fulfilment of God's word in Genesis 8:22, and
therefore the word of God in my own life would be
fulfilled as well. What a wonderful God. I do not know
what word you are trusting God for, if you have not
written it down, please write it down carefully because it
is going to be fulfilled in your life in the name of Jesus. It
is so certain because in heaven there is no limit to God's
blessings, there is no limit to God's snowfall. Join the
snowy day crew!